Economics After Marx

Economics After Marx

Dr. Rammanohar Lohia

ANAMIKA PUBLISHERS & DISTRIBUTORS (P) LTD.
4697/3, 21A, Ansari Road, Daryaganj, New Delhi 110002
Phones: 23281655, 23270239; Fax. : 011-27868035
e-mail: anamikapublishers@yahoo.co.in

First Published 2010

ISBN 978-81-7975-268-5

PRINTED IN INDIA

Published for Samajwadi Sahitya Sansthan, Delhi 110091 by Anamika Publishers & Distributors (P) Ltd., 4697/3, 21A, Ansari Road, Daryaganj, New Delhi - 110002. Typeset by Aadil Printographics, Delhi 110092 and Printed at Nagri Printers, Delhi.

Why This Book?

In the beginning of his political career, when Dr. Rammanohar Lohia was editing *The Congress Socialist*, he criticised Gandhi's village industry programme, in an article and sent the copy of the magazine to Gandhi, asking for his comments. Gandhi wrote back: "You must never expect me to write because I find that you have not the slightest patience with your opponent's views". Lohia apologized and in return received Gandhi's blessings. Lohia later confessed that "it is really a grave disease not to listen to the opponents". He said: "If one may not find it easy to accept the viewpoint of an opponent, one should at least listen to it carefully and understand what he has to say and that is a faculty which we are singularly losing in the modern world".

Ironically, Lohia had himself to suffer this kind of intolerance on the part of his opponents throughout his life. He was ignored, ridiculed, abused and even physically harmed by Jawaharlal Nehru's admirers and official and unofficial operators under his and his successors' regimes, because he opposed Nehru's policies and actions on the ground of betrayal of Mahatma Gandhi as well as the freedom struggle. Such was the vicious grip of Nehru's charm over the middle classes, especially the intellectuals who controlled all newspapers, universities and other centres of learning, that Lohia's writings, even though they were full of refreshing originality and world-class philosophical thought, remained totally ignored. One could understand if only his Hindi writings were given this 'untouchable' treatment, since Hindi and Indian languages were anathema to these intellectuals, but his English writings were also ignored and treated like proscribed writings.

It is tragic for India and also for whole mankind that a person like Lohia, who was among the most fertile and original thinkers of the twentieth century such as Mahatma Gandhi, Albert Einstein, Bertrand Russel, Bernard Shaw, Scott Buchanan etc. and who struggled for and lived by the highest values of human society, should remain un-read and un-appreciated among the intellectuals of his time and about half a century after his death, because of an 'undeclared' ban on his writings by the ruling elite of this country. It is like pronouncement of banishment (even death sentence) on a thinker-activist by the popular dictator and his heirs, accepted and endorsed by the intellectuals and thinkers all over the world. However, the thought could never be suppressed even in deluges. If the Greek thinkers could stir a new awakening in Italy and Europe after several hundred years and Vedic and Upanishadic thought could bring about the great Indian renaissance of the nineteenth century after several thousand years, Lohia's writings could also inspire a search for a new human civilization. With this faith in the immortality of the word (*shabda Brahma*) I undertook the task of collecting, editing and reprinting the works of Dr. Lohia without any help from the establishment which tried to suppress his thoughts in as best a manner as it could.

While doing this work it struck me that his essay 'Economics After Marx' should be published separately in the form of a small book, so that it is made available to scholars as well as general readers on low price, who can then judge for themselves how relevant this essay is for understanding the present crisis of capitalism.

MASTRAM KAPOOR

Economics After Marx

[During the open Rebellion of 1942-43 against British rule, when Socialists were in prison or being hunted, and Communists waged their "Peoples' War" in companionship with the foreign masters, the doctrine of Marxism appalled me with its wide range of contradictory applications. To recover its truth and demolish its untruth became my desire. Of four aspects planned, economics, politics, history and philosophy, I was halfway through the economic when the police got me.

Since then this style of inquiry and expression has ceased to interest me. No man's thought should be made the centre of a political action; it should help but not control. Acceptance and rejection are varying forms of blind worship. I believe that it is silly to be a Gandhian or Marxist and it is equally so to be an anti-Gandhian or anti-Marxist. There are priceless treasures to learn from Gandhi as from Marx, but the learning can only be done when the frame of reference does not derive from an age or a person.

Researchers must still inquire into a man's thought, particularly if the man is Marx or Gandhi. The pages that follow are thoroughly incomplete, and no change has been made since they were written. But error is also a source of knowledge. I only hope that I have made some significant statements so as to titillate some man of greater talent and industry into inquiry. In any event, these pages, I hope, show the need of an economic thought different from any that exists today, that will turn the whole world into a gay unity of equal welfare.]

Communism began as a programme of social justice. Its basis was the achieving of a classless society. Like other programmes of social justice, it was early faced with greed and ignorance and the sarcasm of those who denounce everything great as unpractical and impossible. It therefore elaborated a whole system of philosophy, history, and economy. The fact that its first philosopher was a German of the 19th century might have played a part. In any case the elaboration of an entire system of thought in furtherance of a concrete programme of human improvement is nothing new of history; Vedism, Buddhism, Christianity, Liberalism have gone through a similar phase. What was new in the elaboration of communism was its claim to being scientific, its assertion that it was not a moral law but a causal law. Communism, so claims its philosophy, is a necessary conclusion of the development of capitalism; the classless society must come. Around this claim has arisen a whole code of laws. This code formulated by Marx has produced such a powerful effect that communism and Marxism[1] have become synonymous, that all socialist and communists are in various degrees influenced by it. A study of this system of laws should preferably begin in the realm of capitalist economy, to which it is nearest in scope and about which it is likely to have made the least errors. A summary of the principles and the laws of capitalist development as formulated by Marxism must first be made.

The principle of capitalist development lies in the fact that labour is a commodity like any other commodity. Capitalists buy labour in order that they may with its help produce other commodities for sale. But labour, unlike other commodities, carries within itself two contradictory values. Every other commodity has a single consistent value, the time that is socially necessary to produce it. Labour has indeed this value,

1. Sometimes known as Marxism-Leninism, as Lenin was the first man to put Marxism into practice in a State, and also made partial additions to its general theory.

which is measured by such food and clothing and other requirements of the labourer as are effective in a given capitalist phase. The labourer works and is given his feed so that he may work again. What is given as his "feed" in any particular period is his wages. This is one value of labour, its exchange value, the value of its reproduction, its wages. But labour has another value, its use-value to the capitalist who buys it. The capitalist pays for the labour power of the worker but receives in return all the goods produced by it. From among these goods, a part goes towards the wages of the workers, but another remains as the profit of the capitalist; the labourer's day is split up into two parts, one of which produces wages and another profits. Herein lies the source of all capitalist profits and not in other transactions, for labour is the sole creator of value. In his drive for profits, the capitalist, indeed, tries to make use of machines and improve them in order that he may turn labour power to better account. Machines do not produce better profits; it is mechanized labour that does so. Clearly, therefore, the dynamic of capitalist development lies in the contradiction between the value and the use-value of labour, between wages and produce. This contradiction is the source of surplus value, which makes up the entire profits[2] of the capitalist system. In the career of surplus value can be discerned a whole series of laws of capitalist production and development.

Capital leads to further accumulation of capital. Surplus value or capitalist profit is used for improved machinery and joint labour, which in their turn produce increased surplus value. This is the law of capital accumulation.

Under capitalism, however, production and circulation cannot keep pace with each other. More is produced than can be bought, because productivity of labour and profits continually increase while wages remain comparatively fixed. There is thus a lag between the production and the purchasing

2. Not to be confused with the profits of the entrepreneur. These are the sum of the rent, interest and high earnings of the entire system.

power of a population, which causes crisis in industry. This is the law of the periodic crises of capitalism.

More capital is put into making heavy and intricate machinery, into building the means of production. This tides over the crisis for a while, for it does not immediately lead to increased production, but it lays the basis for a higher productivity in the near future. The organic composition of capital increases, the rate of profit falls, large-scale production increases, smaller capitalists are thrown out, and capitalism changes into monopoly capitalism. This is the law of concentration of capital or of large-scale and monopoly production.

While capital accumulates and concentrates, large sections are turned into the workless, the reserves of industry, and the workers themselves become increasingly poorer. This is the law of pauperization and of accumulation of poverty.

At the same time, the working class is increasingly unified and becomes conscious of itself, by virtue of the fact that it works co-operatively and in large numbers in the big-scale monopolist industries. This is the law of socialization of labour.

Passing through these laws of development, the contradiction between the price of labour and its produce assumes sharp forms. It becomes the contradiction between capitalist appropriation and socialized production, between old relations and expanding forces, between monopoly capitalists and an angry, numerous, socialized working class. The class struggle enters its last phase, when the capitalist husk is burst asunder by the working class. This is known as the law of the class struggle, leaving to the dictatorship of the proletariat.

To these laws must be added yet another on the general crisis of capitalism, when there are no longer any alternating periods of boom and depression in industry. In this period of general and continuing crisis, there are imperialist wars, general exhaustion of capitalism and the victory of the world working class. This is the law of the general crisis of capitalism leading to imperialist wars and the law of the World Revolution.[3]

In his well-known passage establishing how "the expropriators are expropriated," Marx has in a broad sweep defined these "immanent laws of capitalist production" as the "centralization of capital—purposive application of science to the improvement of technique, means of production economized—by social labour, a progressive diminution in the number of the capitalist magnates and a corresponding increase in the mass of poverty, oppression enslavement—a working class which grows ever more numerous, and is disciplined, unified and organized by the very mechanism of the capitalist mode of production." These Marxist laws of capitalist development do not merely possess an interest for the scholar. Although only a few care to read them except as catechisms and fewers still to understand them as a whole, socialists of all description, Marxists, neo-Marxists, anti-Marxists, base their thinking and action on one or the other of these laws, particularly on their source, the general history of the contradiction between the value and the use-value of labour-power.

A vast literature confirming or refuting these laws has arisen. It is largely a literature of barren controversy. We must approach these laws, not to confirm or to deny, but to understand the process of capitalist development.

Let us see how far these laws have been unable to include or have gone against major facts of capitalist development.

---

3. In the elaboration of this law, Engels and Lenin have played a greater part than Marx. Although 26 years before the 1914 war Engels foresaw "the creation of the conditions for the final victory of the working class" through the "general exhaustion" of capitalism in a war, it was left to Lenin and his theoreticians to deepen the law of the periodic crisis into the general crisis of capitalism and of the World Revolution. Should the World Revolution not materialize 60 years after Engel's prediction and 30 years after Lenin's and should world capitalism recover sufficiently from its exhaustion to be able to wage a third world war, what further laws would be elaborated is difficult to tell.

The first casualty is the law of pauperization and of accumulating poverty. It would be useless to deny that, until well after 70 years of the formulation of this law by Marx and 25 years after the first formations of the big concentrations of capital, the proletariat in capitalist countries was not only not pauperized, not growing poorer, but was steadily improving its conditions of living. In fact, German economists were able to assert that, in place of the proletarianization of the middle class and the pauperization of large sections, which Marx had predicted, a steady bourgeoisification of the proletariat was taking place.[4] British economists could point to the black-coated worker. Communists tried to deny these facts and formulas by the astrologer's wait-and-see. There was no such astrological hocus-pocus in Marx's formulations. Pauperization was a necessary consequence of capital accumulation; accumulating poverty was a necessary consequence of monopoly capital; why should 30 years or even 10 elapse before the necessary consequences appear? There must be a reason for it. In fact, sectional poverty and pauperization did appears in the capitalist countries 10 years after the end of the 1914 war, but were again partly overcome. To say that capitalist governments overcame poverty by works programmes and war industries is to state a moral fact, but it is no answer to the "immanent" ability of capitalism to preserve itself from pauperization. Socialist theory must be able to pick up these loose ends, find them a formula and reconcile with facts.

This weakness of Marxist theory in explaining the absence of poverty under capital accumulation has tended to blunt its understanding of what is otherwise a correct description of the industrial crises in capitalism. Industry throughout the 19th century suffered from periodic crises, but quite as periodically got out of them. The main Marxist explanation for these crises,

4. The reader must pardon the use of these terms which communism and the German language have put into the mouth of large numbers but which have no further use except as means of re-education.

as also for their overcoming, lies in the internal structure of capitalism, the conflict between the improving means of production and the constant purchasing power.[5] It is not possible that on this basis capitalism, which is said now to have entered its general crisis, may endure in this state as it endured in its periodic crises and may possibly, while dying out in one country, reappear in another?

As to the law of socialized production, it must be admitted

5. A vast lore has been written on these crises, their periodicity and nature, their causes and so forth. Attempts have been made to number these crises and the regular intervals at which they have occurred. We may also not worry overmuch about the university professors' characterization of these as monetary crisis, production crisis, crisis in confidence, and so forth, for such categories express external forms and do not go to the root of the matter. Marx partly goes to the root when he traces these crises to the conflict between production and consumption, between the higher yield of mechanized labour-power and the constant or decreasing total wages of the working class. But then Marx traces the overcoming of these crises to the same source which is their cause. He and his disciples emphasize the period of improvement in the means of production, building better machinery, and so forth, during which goods of consumption do not immediately appear on the market but wages are still paid. They indeed drop phrases about the pressing of the peasantry, improvement in agriculture, enmeshing of the whole world in the capitalist net, but these facts have not been properly digested in the general Marxist theory on industrial crises. In fact, capitalist politicians and economists have elaborated a medicine-book for industrial crises, and this is none other than the New Deal, works programmes, war industries, and perhaps in an unwilling measure, war, followed by post-war reconstruction. Quite a few of these works programmes like draining of marshes, fighting malaria, building of town halls for assemblies, do not at all enter the consumption market but add to the health and entertainment of the people and also pay out wages to the labourers. Even among the means of production a distinction is made between the machines to manufacture machines which enter into consumption at a late state and the machines which do so earlier. The industry of housing on a capitalist-cum-municipal basis can also tide over a crisis for some time, as it does not immediately enter the market. Capitalism is grouping towards various combinations of industries which produce no or slow effect on the market. Unless the undigested facts of socialist theory on crises are properly understood, we are forced to look upon the capitalist crises, periodic or general, as upon the simple cold, highly unpleasant but not fatal.

that monopoly capital and large-scale enterprises have appeared. What has not taken place is the wiping out of the small capitalist. In fact, the number of small capitalists, either as shareholders in the large undertakings or as owner-managers on their own, has increased. In the same manner, although socialization of labour in the limited sense of thousands of workers working cooperatively in a single establishment has taken place, what has not taken place is their unification. Aside from the technical and managerial classes, the free professions, and the clerical classes, the workers themselves are cut up into a hierarchy of skilled workers, unskilled workers, seasonally employed and their differing wages have turned the predicted solidarity of the working class into a piety-reality.[6]

The worst trick played by history on the Marxist laws of capitalist development lies in the fact that the Revolution took place not in Germany,[7] where it was expected, nor in any other developed country of western Europe, but in Russia. According to the "immanent laws of capitalist development," the capitalist husk was to burst asunder where it proved incompatible with the socialization of labour and the concentration of capital. How this law of the class struggle made an arbitrary leap still remains unexplained and undigested by Marxist theory. Trotsky's explanation that the capitalist chain snapped at its weakest link is indeed a graphic phrase, perhaps true, but an entire denial of the communist teaching on

6. Of late, books from the Marxist angle have appeared on the treason of the technical and free professions, salaried classes, the white-collar worker. Unable to understand why they should be so numerous or powerful, Marxism in Europe alternates between looking upon them as annexe of the bourgeoisie and wooing them as its own allies.
7. For 70 years from the publication of the Communist Manifesto to the Russian Revolution, Marxists, including Lenin, expected the revolution to take place in western Europe, particularly Germany. An odd reference by Marx or Lenin to the possibility of a revolution first in Russia or elsewhere is no more than a side-remark. The prophecy was about Germany and western Europe. For 70 years Marxists lived on this prophecy and after the brief interlude of the Russian revolution returned to it again.

capitalism. Where is the capitalist chain to break? At its most developed link, says Marx; at its weakest link, says Trotsky; and, between these two with various other shades, communism will of course always be right. Lenin's explanation denies Marx as much as Trotsky's does. Lenin explains the Russian revolution by the active role of the Bolshevik Party. With a slight change, in that the Party is now called the Party of Lenin-Stalin, Marxists have memorized this explanation. How this final activity of the class struggle flew out of its iron laws nobody has cared to explain on any scientific basis. In fact, this was not necessary, for Soviet Russia and the Third International soon enough turned their attention again to western Europe as the centre of the world revolution. The master's teaching proved greater than the big fact of the revolution. Marxists are apparently determined to prove, even at the cost of the world revolution itself, that humanity will reach its highest foreseeable development first in Europe.

Marxism is quite accurate in its findings on capital accumulation, correct from one angle on questions of industrial crises, of monopoly and socialization of labour, but factually wrong in the spheres of accumulating poverty, causal class struggle, and the world revolution. Whence comes this conflict between its insight into production and the blind spots regarding circulation? It is not as if poverty and pauperism did not arise or that the centres of class struggle and world revolution could not be located; it is also not that Marx and his disciples were unaware of the relevant facts; it is this that Marxism was not strong enough to digest these facts and weave them into its general theory on capitalism. Let us first get at the relevant facts.

Capitalism first arose in England during the second half of the eighteenth century. The pre-capitalist massings of silver were due as much to the plunder of Spanish ships and Bengal revenues as to the throwing out of farmers from common lands in Britain herself. The first industry to employ machinery, which is the technical basis of capitalism, was textiles. Hardly had this Lancashire industry begun when it had to look out for a dynamic outside its own country, and found it in India. British textiles did not overcome Indian textiles in an economic way. When one of the British parliamentary commissions pointed out that "the wares of Lancashire were bleached with the dry bones of Indian weavers," it did not mean that Indian artisans could not stand competition with British manufactures. Aside from whatever measures were adopted for direct attack upon Indian weavers, the East India Company and its servants by taking the monopoly of internal trade into their own hands were able to dictate what goods should or should not flow in the normal trade channels.[8] The victory of British textiles over Indian textiles was political; the dynamic that Lancashire industry, at its very start, got out of India was due to Britain's rule. Once again, as soon as the first heavy industry of rail-and-engine manufacture is set up in England around the middle of the nineteenth century, it has to get an immediate dynamic from India. It gets that not only by way of the large numbers of engines, rails and other materials used in India but also by way of capital investments in Indian railways which bear a guaranteed minimum interest.[9] This dynamic of Indian railways was continued to act on British engineering industries, in fact, on all of British capitalism, in manifold ways. It need hardly be pointed out that the immense growth

8. To suggest that machine-manufacturers must inevitably drive out hand-manufacturers is here irrelevant. We are concerned with the course of history as it has actually developed and not as one or another theoretician can conceive it to do. History's record shows that, unsupported by British rule over India, not the Indian artisans, but the Lancashire industry would have died in its infancy.
9. This is perhaps the most remarkable financial transaction in world history, unless another one is in the making, according to which British investors got a guaranteed half-yearly interest; and, whenever profits rose above this, got them too. Incidentally, the problem is not whether railway development was a boon to India; the fact is that without British-ruled Indian railways the British railroad industry could hardly have gone beyond an infantile stage. Britain did not give railways to India; India gave Britain her railways and the engineering industry. History is full of such truths which seems to go counter to outward appearances.

of commercial agriculture in India during the latter part of the nineteenth century and after, in the shape of jute, tea, cotton, oil-seeds, and the by-products of hides, pumped a much-needed impetus into British capitalism, sometimes by way of the German and Japanese capitalisms. This commercialization of agriculture took place on the imperial-colonial level, on the level of pauper-wages to landless labour, as in Assam and poverty earnings to farmers, as in Bengal, U.P., and Bihar, except in very limited case of some cotton farmers. Once again when British capitalism was faced at the end of the 1914 war with what has come to be known as a general crisis, Indian railroads alone rushed to its rescue by ordering goods worth a billion rupees and more.[10] This rapid survey of British capitalism has brought us to the conclusion that imperialism and capitalism are of joint origin and development. A similar development can be traced through the career of German capitalism, either by way of sharing in the Austrian, British and French imperial expansion or on its own.[11]

On the surface, American development will seem to have gone a different way. Actually, capitalist development in the United States has needed an identical imperial dynamic, has made use of the same elements as Britain. England used already populated countries like India for her capitalist development. These two elements, a population and a territory, were similarly made use of by American capitalism. The

10. Already, in the midst of the 1939 war, orders for locomotives worth Rs. 42 crores have been placed, and unless something goes wrong more will of course follow.

11. The commercial activity of the Hansa towns like Hamburg, as of the East India Company or of the crafts and guilds, is pre-capitalism. Marxists emphasize, and quite properly, that capitalism should not be confused with other forms of exploitation which might bear some resemblance to it. German capitalism begins around the middle of the nineteenth century with the Customs Union and the Listian economy according to which free trade has meaning only after unequal historical conditions have been removed, (to the European, German or British, western Europe is his world), and it really comes into shape with the Bismarckian unification of Germany.

territory was new and contiguous, and the population was got from Europe. This territorial expansion took place over the larger part of the nineteenth century. To understand this one has only to look at a map of the United States as it stood at the beginning and as it got to be at the end of the nineteenth century. All the Mid-western States, the Prairie States, the Border States, the Eastern States, a territory larger than India, were the result of this expansion.[12] The problem of man-power for these large territories was also solved in an imperial way. No less than 30 million European paupers[13] came into the United States during the century and settled in its factories or on its lands. Each fresh batch of immigrants stood, at least for a generation, in an imperial-colonial relationship with the older inhabitants, until it got Americanized. That imperialism and capitalism have jointly developed in capitalist history is clearly established by the American case. The results of this joint development inside the frontiers of what is now a single country and a single nation are indeed fundamentally different from those of the British. How American capitalism overcame its twin is a brave story of the Jeffersons, Jacksons and Lincolns, but whether this was due to the new and robust American nationality or to the fullness of natural resources and a corresponding labour yield, and whether this may not yet lead to an imperial-colonial relationship on a world scale is not within our present scope. It need hardly be added that

12. The old inhabitants of these territories, the Red Indians, were almost exterminated in wars and skirmishes. For one big chunk, which was finally acquired by purchase, the United States President sent his negotiators armed, quite in the modern style, with two sets of orders, to buy if possible, else to wage a shooting war.

13. The story of these paupers goes counter to Marx's analysis. Until capitalism arose in England and France paupers came principally from these two countries. Graphic stories are told of how British men kidnapped British women in the streets of London and of marriage-at-first-sight bargainings in the New Work Harbour. The growth of capitalism in England put an end to it. Then came the turn of Germany, Italy and Ireland before they turned capitalist. Last came the Negro labour had been brought as slaves in the earlier century.

Japanese capitalism began as a system of industries rapidly built chiefly out of government revenues, and it could therefore wait for two decades or so before it too went the imperial way.

In face of this wide wealth of facts, how anyone could have suggested that imperialism is the last stage of capitalism is beyond comprehension.[14] Imperialism not only appears at the first stage of capitalism but goes on developing with it. Capitalism seeks it external dynamic, one might say, even before it is born and, insatiable in this search, it gobbles up

14. Lenin has devoted a whole book to the thesis that imperialism is the last stage of capitalism. This astounding phrase is meant to convey the fact of increasing capital investments in the colonies and semi-colonies. If we limit imperialism to capital investments, what of the factory goods that capitalism right at its start forced on the colonies and has been forcing ever since, not to talk of the other tribute of salaries and pensions and currency tricks. Moreover, even as capital investments go, Britain had already made the first of these in India around 1850, very much in the middle stage of her capitalism. Lenin's tables of statistics of increasing capital investments in the colonies from decade to decade have no more than a book-keeping significance on this issue, for if colonial investments have increased, so has capitalist production. Keener students will find it worth their while to publish the respective ratios of Britain's total industrial production to her colonial investments and to her exports in the decade 1850-60 or 1860-70, and also in the decade 1900-10. If Lenin had made such a study he would have found that the total volumes of each of the three categories increase but the ratios are not vastly altered. Such a misuse of the term "imperialism" has greatly obscured the fact of joint capitalist-imperialist development and instead of correcting Marx's theory on capitalism has further confused it. As a Russian, Lenin was probably influenced by the fact that his nation's first contact with capitalism was by way of West-European investments and he might also have wanted to give a clever turn to the phrase "finance-capital" popularized by Hilferding. Curiously enough, Indian Socialists have also unthinkingly repeated this phrase. What Lenin and these other have probably meant to convey is that capitalism has already covered the whole world in its net and therefore it must either war and die or find a new dynamic in the more intensive exploitation of the colonies. It is also possible that in their anxiety to discover a proletariat in every country on Marx's pattern of the class struggle they have tended to equate imperialism with large imperialist investments.

one country after another. First Bengal and the Americas, then the whole of India, and on to China and Egypt, thence to South America and Malaya and Java and Burma and the great continent of Africa; the limits of the world are reached. No single dynamic lasts capitalism for long; it is soon stabilized, and, with an almost magic resourcefulness it uses the old dynamic for the conquest of a new one, Bengal for United Provinces, India for China and Burma, and so forth. Not only does an old dynamic continue to give capitalism a part of the needed surplus for home-production; not only does it produce armies and war-chests; it also yields labour-power, for instance, Chinese and Indians in Malaya, Indians in East Africa, Fiji, and such far-off lands as Trinidad. If ever the world is able to look back upon capitalism and its playtime—the nineteenth century and after—without the heat of battle, it will contemplate with wonder this cruel and unscrupulous, but nevertheless, cleverest scoundrel of all history.

But now the limits of the world are reached. Capitalism's insatiable expansiveness has come up against a dead wall. How will it, or can it at all, solve this contradiction between its expansive need and a limited world? But that is a question of its most recent development and its future, which we will take up at the proper place. Meanwhile, let us look at another aspect of the career of capitalism through history which is sharply related to this contradiction. Once upon a time there was but one capitalism in the world, Britain's, for five decades or so of the 18th and 19th centuries. In its *herrscher gait* through the world it showed its superiority in war and its wealth in peace. It was also willing to help in the birth of cousins. Culture-capitalisms were born.[15] By the first decade of our century

15. Like a culture-pearl, which incidentally is not an artificial pearl, capitalism is sterile on colonial soil, whatever be the volume of its trade with or investments in the colonies; if this were not so, we should have had a capitalism much sooner in India than we had it in Japan or Germany or even the U.S.A. Capitalism sells the machines to manufacture machines to

(*Contd. …*)

there were four such major capitalisms besides Britain's: German, American, Japanese and French. This growth of culture-capitalisms has further sharpened the conflict between capitalist expansiveness and the limited world. We are thus living in an age which has come to be known as the epoch of imperialist wars, and which with greater appropriateness can be called the epoch of capitalist wars. Can capitalism scotch the birth of new culture-cousins? Can it lay low some to its existing ones? Can the world, instead of going socialist, remain capitalistic by a process of stagnation or seesaw? These are some of the intriguing questions of future development. For the present, let us weave the results of our inquiry into a correct theory of capitalist development. We have found the fact of joint capitalist-imperialist development. We have found the fact of the growth of culture-capitalisms. We have finally found the fact of multiplying capitalisms within a territorially limited imperialism.

The question of whether capitalism is at all possible without imperialism may be briefly answered with the strict understanding that in history so far there has been no capitalism without imperialism and that, therefore, it relates to the problematic future and asks for prophecy. Clearly, capitalism, depending upon an exclusive internal dynamic, theoretically improbable in a vast country with a vast population, will have to bear two burdens at the same time, the joint capitalist-imperialist burdens. Most likely it will crash under these

---

cousins, that is, to such *free countries* as have the forces for capitalist growth; one might almost say that it is conscious of pedigree and wants no nonsense of half-breeds. That these cousins alternate between being partners and enemies of each other is rather unfortunate; but it is better than having a litter of children who might all come of age. But this fact of culture-capitalisms opens out other vistas of inquiry. Is it possible that any new system of economy that establishes its superiority in war and obvious wealth has a tendency to produce cousins? Is it possible that the submerged countries in any world-phase yearn to produce such a culture system? Is it finally possible that even opposing systems, for instance, the socialist to the capitalist, tend to produce culture-pearl traits of each other?

burdens; most certainly it will cause impoverishment on a hitherto unknown scale.

Let us now reconstruct the theory of capitalist development. Marx's initial fallacy was to have examined capitalism in the abstract, to have wrenched it outside of its imperialist context. Marx was not unaware of imperialist exploitation and his disciple, Lenin, was even more keenly aware of it. But imperialism is with both Marx and Lenin a tumour of capitalism, an odorous after-growth, and this has at best awakened an unintelligent concern for the colonial races. Marxism has therefore not been able to give a consistent theory of capitalist development. Its picture of capitalism is that of a West-European entity, with the later additions of the American and Japanese forms, more or less wrenched out of the world, more or less developing internally. All the dynamic of capitalism is placed within its internal structure, in the contradiction between the value and the use-value of labour-power, between the working class and the capitalist class of the self-same structure. Marx's capitalism was that of a self-moving West-European circle, no doubt causing great repercussions in the outside world, but the principle and laws of its own movement were exclusively internal. Marxism to this day remains stuck in this picture, no doubt formulating laws about these outside repercussions, but wholly unable to state the basic interacting principle of the two, internal and external, movements of capital. Socialism must forever shatter this unreal Marxist picture. In its place must arise a picture of two circles, one placed inside the other, the inner circle representing the free capitalist structures with their dynamic in the contradiction between capitalist profits and mechanized labour, the other circle representing the colonial economy of the rest of the world with its dynamic between imperial exploitation and colonial labour, the rim of the inner circle possessing an enormously porous capacity to suck into itself the dynamic of the outer. This is the only way in which we can join up the capital-labour dynamic with the empire-colony dynamic and arrive at a consistent understanding of the development of capitalism.[16]

The communist theory of capitalist development starts with the contradiction between the value and the use-value of labour and with the surplus value thus generated. The career of this surplus value reveals the further laws of capitalist development. All this needs to be restated, in the light of our investigations, both as to labour's value and its use-value. Labour is not an abstract thing, although Marx made it so. In spite of their horror of idealistic concepts, communists have continued to treat labour as an ideal, abstract entity. Actually, labour under capitalism has shown two forms, which differ so widely from each other that lumping them in one category can never give us a proper understanding. Labour has been either imperial or colonial, and there have been vast divergences in their values. It is for these divergences that communism has had to evolve the concept of the socially effective requirements of labour. But its basic concept of the necessary requirements of labour[17] has stood in the way and

---

16. Some persons will here remarks that the two dynamics are present in Marxist studies of capitalism. Nobody questions that. The issue is whether the two dynamics are so interconnected and the basic laws of this interconnection so discovered as to give a consistent understanding of the world. It is this interconnection that socialism must study. For a type of intellect which can only be satisfied by crude evaluations, let it be said here that of all other Europeans, Karl Marx is the greatest economist of European history. But we must not be satisfied with that, for we need the economics of world history.
17. University economics has tried to understand the present distribution of wealth among various countries of the world, and is preserving this understanding with the help of a few concepts. Let us examine the major concepts.
    (a) *Necessary Requirements of Labour:* The requirements of labour are supposed to vary from country to country. Colder climates like those of England and Germany are believed to necessitate richer food, better housing, more clothing and so forth, than tropical climates like those of Africa and India. As a result of these higher calories of food and so forth, labour in colder climates is also believed to be more productive.

(*Contd. ...*)

prevented a richer understanding of the newer and correct concept. There are no necessary requirements of labour; at least, they have no economic relevance except in periods of famine. Human labour has shown a remarkable tenacity to live and work, and its requirements have varied from the minimum of 2 annas a day for colonial labour to that of Rs. 4 a day for imperial labour. This shows that requirements of labour are dictated, not nature or physique, but by history.

Historical development has dictated that a colonial labourer shall keep himself upon the brink of starvation and work, while nature has shown its marvellous elasticity in how very little is needed to keep a man alive and enable him to turn up for work day after day. We thus find that there are two distinct values or wages of labour, those effective in the

---

Thus the teaching has sprung up of the greater productivity and also the greater requirements of labour in colder climates. This teaching is wholly erroneous. There is no reason why the German should not be able to make do with the food of the Tibetan and carry a charcoal fire stove bound to his back or live the winters of his entire lifetime in a single Eskimo coat. There is likewise no reason why the Indian can naturally labour without electric fans and air-conditioning and fruit juice and similarly nourishing food to fight the rigours of a tropical sun. If climate has any economic relevance, the coal fire and central heating of colder climates has its opposite number in the fans and air-conditioning of warmer climates, the heavy meat-and-drink diet, in the fruit-and-milk diet, so that one might legitimately say that the requirements of labour in warmer climates are naturally higher than those in colder climates. But to be able to say that one would require an excess of political power in warmer climates as compared to that in colder. In fact, Europeans have in the past been able to do with Eskirm coats and without baths and the like. Quite obviously, therefore, there are no such things as the necessary requirements, of labour; there are only such requirements as varying political fortunes have been bestowed upon this country or that. The Indian peasant who is today supposed naturally to sleep in the open and work may as naturally be supposed, in a different political climate, to require for his labour a pukka house lighted and ventilated by electricity. This brings us to the question of what labour produces.

(b) *Productivity of Labour:* The teaching that credited labour in colder

(*Contd. ...*)

imperial countries and those effective in the colonies. This distinction between imperial labour and colonial labour and their respective wages is of the utmost importance for a proper understanding of the source of surplus value. Likewise, the concept of the use-value, the produce, of labour remains abstract and meaningless unless it is understood in the context of joint capitalist-imperialist development. In the current produce of labour in West-European factories appears the saved labour of many generations of colonials. Economists, including communists, are wrong in crediting this entire produce to imperial labour and in using pompous phrases about the higher productivity of labour in Europe as compared to Asia or Africa. Labour, on the whole, uses the same muscle-power and skill everywhere, and what appears as the higher produce of

---

countries with a higher productivity by virtue of the climate itself is so patently untrue that it has almost been given up. It is now clothed in different garments. Such concepts as the lack of proper food or of training and skill are introduced to explain the low produce of colonial labour. Indian economists and businessmen make free use of these concepts. When, for instance, the low yield of the Indian steel worker is compared with the high yield of the British steel worker, this is naturally put down to the ill-fed and ill-trained condition of the former. Thus do our capitalists and economists hide their own shame and dishonour. For the West-European capitalist economy, Karl Marx proved conclusively that the concepts of skilled and unskilled labour are highly transitory: what is skilled today may become unskilled tomorrow and the labour that can be got dirt-cheap today may require good wages tomorrow. Let us look at our own rickshaw driver. It is difficult to imagine a more exacting or a more skilled type of labour. In like manner, if there were some way to measure the labour-power spent by the Indian metal-worker and by his British opposite number, it would be found that the former has performed no less exacting labour. The economic fact is that the ill-fed Indian worker or peasant has to do as exacting labour, in some cases even more so, and use as much of his muscle-power as the better-fed British worker. Is it then the higher skill of the European labourer that does the trick? We have already commented upon the skill of the rickshaw driver, than which there can be nothing higher in the steel industry. The motor or bus driver in India is certainly as skilled as his opposite number in Europe.

(*Contd. …*)

imperial labour is directly due to the many generations of imperial-colonial division of labour in the world. One might almost say that the ghosts of hundreds of millions of colonial toilers are invisibly moving the machines in imperial factories. The highly elaborate machinery and its continuing improvement in capitalist countries are due, in large part, to the surplus value created in colonial firms and mines. The continuing use of the productive capacity of these factories is also due, in large part, to the vast masses of colonial toilers who buy their produce. In this welter of a current production that carries with it many entangled skeins of history and of two distinctive value of labour, the old formula that capitalist development has proceeded with the contradiction between labour's wages and its produce has become meaningless.

Perhaps what is meant is a particular type of skill required for a particular type of machinery, there being no suggestion that any one is higher than the other. Even here it will be difficult to prove how the skill of the rivet-driver in our country differs from that of the British. What may be possible is that adaptation to a particular kind of machinery may require a few years so that the labour that has the earlier run enjoys a short-lived advantage. But conditions are soon equalized. Therefore, despite the concept of ill-fed and ill-skilled labour as an explanation of the low produce in our industry Indian workers use as much, if not more, muscle-power and skill as labour elsewhere. Is it then their own incompetence which Indian capitalists seek to transfer to our labour?

(c) *Capitalist Enterprise:* Capacity to mix in the most profitable proportions the three factors of production, land, labour, and capital, and the readiness to take risks or to break out into unexplored regions of technique and industry are regarded as a part of the entrepreneur's skill in text book economics. Aside from the question of why this skill should get higher profits than, say, the skill of the school teacher, it would be wholly absurd to suggest that the entrepreneur's skill in the more important countries is of higher or lower order. The Indian capitalist is as skilful in the selection of sites for his industries and in marketing as the European; if anything, he is even more skilled in the manipulation of labour. He can also take enormous risks, as evidenced by his bold speculations. This teaching of entrepreneur's skill, whatever may be its role in the internal economy of a country, has absolutely no meaning when applied to distinguish one important

(*Contd. ...*)

If capitalism has extracted surplus value from its home labourers by paying them less than what they produce, upon this extraction has continually acted the far greater surplus value derived from colonial toilers. Do the immensely rich persons and the vast middle classes of England and Germany receive surplus value from home-labour or from colonial labour, and in what ratios? Does not imperial labour itself, at least some of its better-paid ranks, receive a large measure of surplus value extracted from colonial labour? There seems to be only way to get out of this labyrinth. We must forever abandon the habit of examining a country's economic structure as a self-moving entity; we must therefore abandon the Marxist understanding of capitalism as a self-moving West-European entity. Capitalism from its origin to its most recent

---

country from another. What has meaning is another concept, a country's total economic structure which is naturally dependent upon its politics. This explains why the Indian capitalist, while he takes the most fantastic risks in commercial speculation, is wholly crippled when it comes to breaking out into new techniques and industry. On industrial risks he is as dishonourable as the tortoise, probably because he knows that the moment he takes out his head he will be decapitated. It is to this dishonour of a colonial economic structure, and not to the supposed lower yield or lower needs of our labour, nor even to entrepreneur's skill, that our low economic productivity should be traced.

(d) *National Resources:* Attempt is often made to refer to a country's natural resources to explain and justify what in university economics is known as the geographical division of labour. For instance, the presence of humidity in the Lancashire atmosphere, and therefore Manchester textiles are brought in some sort of a mutually beneficial connection with the cotton growing black-soil of Maharashtra. The actual use of artificial sprays in Indian textile mills has completely busted up this connection, for the cost of these sprays is not even an infinitesimal fraction of the earlier two-way freight charges. This does not, however, mean that there are no such things as differing natural resources. It is to these resources that the United States owes, in part, its preponderant position in the world; with 6 per cent of the world's population, it controls nearly 25 per cent of the world's resources. Here again one has to be very careful. The factor of scientific

(*Contd. ...*)

development has moved mainly on the imperial dynamic. So that we may evolve a formula which may grasp at the same time the internal and external dynamics of capitalism, we have to give up the idea of an isolated produce of labour within a single economic structure and replace it instead with the concept of the world's total production averagely distributed over its working population. Thus, the contradiction is not between labour's requirements and its produce, but between the politically effective requirements of labour and the average production of the world for each worker. Surplus value cannot be calculated, nor understood, on the communist basis of the difference between labour's requirements and its produce. Surplus value, wherever it appears and to the extent that it does so, is the difference between the actual

---

inventiveness can almost equalize differing natural resources. The present estimate of a country's resources is made on the basis of factor such as coal, iron, petrol, water-power and so forth, which have already acquired key importance. But one can depend on science to produce petrol out of coal, and sugar out of wood, and if these ersatz industries may with some reason be regarded as a waste in the perspective of world economy, there are remarkable new inventions in fields such as plastics or electronics which open out the prospect of wholly new industries. Firmly entrenched vested interests of iron and steel in the already industrialized counties may make it impossible for the plastics industry to grow, whereas another country with less resources in iron may develop this new industry with great profit to itself. Scientific inventiveness can thus add to the great variety of key natural resources and equalize the differences among various countries. No doubt applied science will have to be more alert and alive and diversified as between one country and another than it has been so far; it must not blindly follow already explored lines. In this way differences in natural resources can be equalized and a country poor on the present showing may even aspire to gain a lead, however short-lived, over others. In order that we can have a really beneficial world trade and obtain a true teaching of the geographical division of labour, science must have unfettered scope in various parts of the world and also make intelligent, human use of its possibilities. Until this is done text book teaching on natural resources must be viewed with suspicion, and be looked upon as a justification of the existing

(*Contd. ...*)

earnings of labour and the per worker world production of the time. It is in the career of this surplus value that the laws of capitalist development can be discerned.

Surplus value, which makes up the entire profits and high earnings of the capitalist system, is derived mainly from colonial farms, fields and mines. The inner imperial circle of the capitalist structure revolves in a way as to draw with great suction the labour-yield of the outer colonial circle. One can quite graphically describe the movements in colonial economy through the past two centuries to now. Four distinct rings inside this circle are discernible. The outermost, and now perhaps the broadest band is composed of landless labour in agriculture, and the suction here has been the strongest. The second, almost equally broad, band of the peasantry, factory

---

geographical division of labour, that is, of imperial structures on the one hand and colonial structures on the other.

We have found that the concepts of the necessary requirements of labour, of the productivity of labour, of capitalist skill and of natural resources, when used to distinguish one country from another, are either meaningless or harmful to proper understanding. To understand world economy, as it is and as it has travelled through the past two centuries, we need such concepts as the politically effective requirements of labour, the productivity of the total economic structure, the imperial-colonial division of labour.

What we have hitherto had as the science of economics are nothing else but the rules of accountancy, industrial management, trade and banking. The science of economics is yet to mature. This is further illustrated by the pitiful use that economics makes of statistics.

Fairly copious statistics are now available of the total annual production in various countries, their national incomes, foreign trade, capital investments, and so forth. What does economics do with them? It just establishes surface ratios. For instance, we know that in a normal year 20 per cent of Britain's production enters into export trade; around 3 per cent comes to India; the total of investment dividends and home charges going out of India do not make over than 2 or 3 per cent of Britain's national income. According to these surface calculations, India contributes, at best, 5 per cent to Britain's national income. The politician, Mr. Churchill, is nearer the truth than these

(Contd. ...)

worker, and such lower middle class as the small trader and the primary school teacher has been sucked at just a slightly less intensive rate. Then comes the rather thin ring of the middle classes which alternates between sucking and being sucked. Last comes the almost invisible streak of monopoly capitalist which appears at a late stage and acquires completely the capitalist quality of seizing the labour-yield of others. This outer colonial circle with its four rings moves as an adjunct of the inner capitalist circle to which it is attached in political and economic slavery. The suction does not abate, and throughout, but more particularly at the point when exhaustion is reached, the outermost bands of landless labour and small peasantry are piled up with the dried bones of starvation and famine. The colonial economies become one vast village to the capitalist

---

calculations of economists are, when he puts down India's contribution to Britain's national income as around 15 to 20 per cent. In fact, it might even be more. For Mr. Churchill is aware that money expressions of economic values greatly obscure the dynamics that go on underneath, that the loss of dynamic in one region leads to losses in other regions, and so forth.

Let us evaluate the statistics of India's foreign trade as the science of economics ought to. We would find that, in a normal year, 5,000 crores of labour-hours spent on our farms and fields are exchanged for 250 crores of labour-hours spent in British factories. German and Japanese factories have also their share. These calculations are easily made. If, out of our production estimated at Rs. 2,000 crores in a normal year, Rs. 100 cores worth of agricultural goods enter our export trade, 1/20th of our entire population, that is, 2 crores of men, have been at the job of producing these exported goods. For the purpose of ensuring complete comparison, the entire population and not the working population is here regarded. At the estimate of 2,500 labour-hours per man per year, we get a total of 5,000 crores labour-hours spent on the production of our exported agricultural goods. Likewise, if out of the British production estimated at Rs. 4,000 crores in a normal year Rs. 100 crores worth of industrial goods enter the export trade, 1/40th of the British population, that is, 10 lakhs of men, have been at the job of producing these exported goods. Thus 250 crores of labour-hours are spent on the production of industrial goods imported into India. This is the real

(*Contd. ...*)

economies. The town-village relationships of exploitation inside a country are nothing compared to this deciding town-village relationship in which three-fourths of mankind is transformed into a village for the benefit of the rest.

With this instrument of an interwoven inner and outer dynamic, we are in a position to understand the other appearances of capitalist development. In particular, the high capitalization of West-European industry is made intelligible. This industry has not only continually got the larger part of its capital from overseas profits, but it has continually found overseas outlets for its produce in goods as well as its capital accumulations. Thanks to the fact that corresponding industries could not be established in the major part of the world, West-European industry could capitalize itself so

---

story, which money statistics of India's foreign trade are so shy of revealing, that the labour of 2 crores of men is exchanged against that of 10 lakhs of men; 5,000 crores of labour-hours are exchanged for 250 crores of labour-hours. It will not do to summon the exploded concepts of labour productivity or of natural resources to explain this fantastic exchange. The concept of the imperial-colonial division of labour, of the productivity of the total economic structure, alone can explain it. Behind this fantastic exchange lies the history of layer upon layer of saved labour from generations of tillers and miners of India, China, Java, Malaya, Africa, South America, and other lands, which has continually been converted into the gigantic machines of England, Germany and Japan.

How then to disentangle the two surplus values, that which capitalism extracts from labour in its home factories and that which it extracts from colonial labour? There is so much of history, so much of continually changing dynamics wrapped up with this problem that one despairs of evolving an adequate mathematical formula. And yet, cannot perhaps this terrific flux of surplus value be grasped by a simple formula, if we bear in mind that labour's use of muscle-power and skill is the same all the world over and, granted equal conditions of technique, would yield equal produce? In fact, university economists who believe in exchange of equal values should have no difficulty in accepting this formula. Let us then convert the world's entire production of a year into the currency of any one country. Care should be taken to convert not the nominal values, but the real values.

(*Contd. ...*)

highly, could become unmistakably monopolistic. The West-European population could never have borne the burden of this heavy capitalization, could neither have created it nor carried it through, not even if they could have distributed their produce on a communist basis.

Just as this heavy capitalization is the outcome largely of overseas dynamic, the overcoming of periodic crises is to be traced to the same source. To say that industrial crises are caused by the lag between a people's production and their purchasing power or that they are overcome by inventions and heavier capitalization is to state some half-truths and outward appearances. Industrial crises, in addition to partially resulting from the capitalist distribution of internal incomes, have more largely been due to the time-lag between the exhaustion of an old imperial dynamic and the discovery of a new one. An old

---

We may then divide this production equally among the world's working population. For the rough calculation that follows the world's entire population is taken into account. In our own currency, this would roughly work out at Rs. 100 per head per year. Whoever receives less than this as his income, and to the extent that he does so, man, woman, or their child, is a contributor to the surplus value of capitalism; whoever receives more than this, and to the extent that he does so, is a recipient. This will perhaps show that nearly 99 per cent of colonial labour and not more than 10 per cent of imperial labour are the victims from whom capitalism extracts its profits, although, perhaps another 10 per cent of imperial labour lives on the margin. The accountants, misnamed economists, will perhaps wilt at this calculation. They might suggest that this calculation steps up India's production exactly double by a magician's trick, and it makes two appear where there is only one. They have to be reminded that the one their eyes are unable to see has for generations been crossing India's frontiers and appearing in the products of West-European and Japanese factories. They have also to be reminded that the spending of muscle-power and skill is the same all the world over, and if it today yields less in India, China or Africa, that is because its previous yields of many generations lie congealed in the machines of other lands.

We can now define surplus value. Labour, whether of the peasant or the factory worker, creates surplus value to the extent that its earnings fall below the average-per-worker world production of its time.

technique of producing goods with a given overseas area for imperialist exploitation tends to produce crisis, until a new overseas area is conquered to enable the use of a new invention.[18] Thus was it possible for capitalism to survive its first crisis and its later periodic crisis, for internal purchasing power could in no event have sufficed for its produce. Thus is it that with the complete conquest of the world and the impossibility of a new imperial dynamic, capitalism has entered the phase of general crisis. It is wholly unable to get out of this phase. Whether it will as a result break asunder or stabilize itself at low levels of wealth will be considered later.

Capitalist crises are often sought to be understood in terms of the rise or fall in the rate of interest. As an outward appearance, it is incontestable that crisis is a period of very low out-turns on capital, that is, almost negligible rates of interest, while boom is a period of high out-turns. It is also true that, after a period of abnormally low out-turns, a new invention for the production of goods used to bring a higher yield on capital. A new composition of capital and labour took place. But this is merely touching the surface of the problem of crises, or even of the rate of interest. Going deeper, we are offered such explanations as that new inventions caused a fall in the costs of production and the price of goods, and, with the increase in population, this gave higher profits to capitalists and thus

---

18. If an attempt were made to pair off Stephenson's steam engine or the Bessemer process or the internal combustion engine with such events as the conquest of Bengal or the opining of the Suez Canal and the consequent commercialization of Indian agriculture or the conquest of Africa, the results would prove that a crisis set in largely as old colonial areas started proving inadequate and capitalism got restored to health with new political or economic annexations. Incidentally, this theory of capitalist crises might mean that such heavy capitalization as in European industry would, even under socialist conditions, be impossible without imperialist exploitation. We will consider this question later.
P.S. —I have now come to believe in the utter impossibility of such heavy capitalization for the whole world, not alone because of the unavailability of imperialist exploitation, but also because most of the retarded two-thirds of the world possesses a tremendous density of population—1952.

restored equilibrium. This is yet not a full explanation. Each boom-making utilization of new inventions and the consequent fall in the costs of production were possible only with the fresh markets of large overseas populations for trade as well as investments. It was this situation that restored capitalist equilibrium and profits, and the new restorations tended to be on lower levels of interest. With the possibility of such new restorations now blocked, capital is faced with the problem of a zero or a minus rate of interest. Capital is faced with its own extinction. This is the problem of the general crisis of capitalism.

While capitalism has progressed through periodic crises in its homelands, it has brought devastating paupery and increasing poverty to the colonies. Landless and starving labour in agriculture has claimed an increasingly higher percentage in the total population. Because of their basic misunderstanding of the dynamic of capitalism, Marxists have looked for increasing impoverishment among imperial labour, whereas they should have looked for it in colonial labour. The history of capitalist development is the history of the increasing poverty of colonial masses and their reduction into starving and landless labour.[19]

---

19. Landless labour in Indian agriculture has risen from being less than 200 of each 1,000 agriculturists at the end of the last century to nearly 400 in each 1,000. This is the most important result of the commercialization of agriculture. Nevertheless, men can still say that India has been enriched through commercial agriculture. It would be hard to find a more obvious stream of blood that has flown from a huge mass of population to a foreign economy or to a section in its own. The receivers of this stream alone can talk of the enriching of the people from whom it is taken. There is no greater collapse of human intelligence than when an Indian or any other colonial repeats parrot-like the Marxist formula that capitalism was at one time progressive but has now ceased to be so. Capitalism has at no time been progressive to the colonial masses; it has increasingly wasted their economic and spiritual welfare. If only someone with sympathy and a historical sense could write "the History of Colonial Labour in India," it would not only be a service to knowledge but would read like a thriller. The materials of such a history may have to be found in the indenture records of

(*Contd. ...*)

The worst sufferers under capitalism are the colonial masses. Presuming the validity of the Communist law of class struggle, there is obvious need to change its basis. Not the working class in capitalist countries, but the colonial masses are the principal grave-diggers of capitalism. Imperial labour can at best be an ally of colonial toilers in the destruction of capitalism. The class of colonial toilers[20] pours its life-blood into the capitalist system from its birth, carries it along through its various phases, and is itself steadily impoverished until it reaches a stage when its own extinction spells the decay of capitalism, while its purposeful rise into manhood ushers in a new world. Whether the class of colonial toilers will do its work well or ill, whether it will allow itself to stay in decay or rise into manhood, will be discussed under the most recent development of capitalism. Suffice it here to say that the future

---

such far-off lands as Fiji and Trinidad; they will have to be ferreted out of the numerous British commissions and reports; old budgets and prices will have to be discovered, and, in part, they may have to be reconstructed out of such evidence as is available from men who are before our eyes fading into skeletons. This might take a whole lifetime, but it would be a great work. Such a history would relate the repeated auctionings of Bengal lands by Hastings, the speedy reduction of craftsmen into landless labourers, the cry for salt and oil, labour's work on rail embankments and roads, to be followed by successive gazes on its flooded fields and its own creation, the story of its fascinating women quickly fading into wrinkles, and gawkiness or of a rare flower picked up by the zamindar's son and the indigo saheb only to be thrown away, the occasional revolts, the resignation and pain of indenture slaves on ramshackle ships and on lands thousands of miles away, the arrival of jute and tea and cotton with Bessemer and the Suez canal with them—the piteous cry for food, famines, the stifled moan, the wondrous victory of the loin cloth over nakedness, the background of the huge factories in foreign lands and their spawns in Bombay, Calcutta and like towns, and through all this story of vanishing food and vanishing cloth, running like a red thread, the disgrace of caste and the songs of Paltu and other Bhagats that spoke of the dissolving happiness in the Great Absolute.

20. Whatever Marxists may say about the impossibility of regarding the colonial toilers as a single class, even under Marx's tests of community, political consciousness, and national organization, the colonial toilers as a whole are more justifiably a class than is the working class of capitalist countries.

of capitalism depends not so much on the behaviour of labour in capitalist countries as on the behaviour of colonial masses. The student of the capitalist future will have his eyes pre-eminently on the political action of colonial toilers.

The Russian revolution fits in very well with this theory of the class-struggle. As a country which by no means formed part of the inner capitalist circle of world economy, but was being gradually brought into the outer colonial circle of the West Europeans, its semi-colonial toilers were yet powerful enough to overthrow the foreign and native systems that spelled their servitude. The capitalist chain snapped where the colonial masses supplied their strongest link. Those desirous of seeing the capitalist chain break again will do well to look for the now strongest link in the class of colonial toilers. Such a breaking may perhaps usher in a real new world, as the snapping link is now no longer semi-colonial but wholly colonial, and vitally necessary to capitalist continuance.

Before we go on to consider the most recent development of capitalism, let us ask ourselves how Marx could have made an inadequate use of his own instrument, and have considered capitalism in its West-European isolation. One is tempted to answer in the Marxian way that, as a limb of European economy, Marx could not see beyond the interests of the European working class. As a philanthropist, he vaguely wanted the whole world to prosper, but the centre of his world with its deciding movements for economic and spiritual welfare was placed in West Europe. This view is further confirmed by the attitude of Marx's critics. They have attacked Marx's theory of capitalist development from various angles such as marginal utility or preference scales and costs of production, but none of them, even as an argument, has pointed out the error of Marx in looking upon imperial labour as the sole creator of value in capitalist factories. Capitalists and communists alike of West-Europe have maintained a singular silence over this division of labour into imperial and colonial and the great consequences of this division to capitalist development through its various phases. One would be tempted to call this conspiracy of thought a reflection of economic interests, but that Asiatic socialists have also been party to it only proves that thinking has perhaps its own laws and its lapses need not always be put down to economic self-interest or the working of class forces.

The recent development of capitalism can be appropriately studied by analyzing West-European economy after the first decade of our century. Apart from the fact that West-Europe until recently decided the destiny of more than half of the human race and was consequently the main determinant in the affairs of capitalism, it has during this period had the strength to involve the whole world in two major wars. In the study of the West-European economy we will be concerned with economic facts, as the thoughts and motives of men, except in so far as they are of economic consequence, will be studied in another connection.

The main source of West-European economic movement in this period has lain in the extremely heavy capitalization to industry and in the fact of multiplying capitalism within a territorially blocked imperialism. The capitalization of West-European industry had, until the first decade of our century, proceeded on the basis of ever-available large chunks of colonial masses and their territories; it needed an expanding world on which to operate. The source of such an expansion is now completely blocked. There are no more new worlds whose colonial masses can act as a dynamic to West-European capitalization. On the contrary, a kind of diminishing returns has begun to operate in the available spheres because of the increasing poverty of colonial masses as well as their obstruction and opposition. All this has produced a chronic condition in West-European capitalization: not only has industry reached the summit of its capacity, and can no longer expand, but it cannot make use of whatever capacity it has already reached. The use of productive capacity fell in the five years of the 1929 depression to nearly three-fourths, and in certain industries it was as low as 50 per cent. Even in the five years immediately preceding the 1939 war, Britain and France could not make full use of their productive capacities. This downward trend in the use of productive capacity was accompanied by downward trends in world trade and employment.[21] West-European capitalism has thus been faced by three kinds of insecurities to its existence; insecurity due to colonial poverty and obstruction; insecurity of internal disorders; and insecurity as a result of competition within its own ranks and from extra-European lands. Due perhaps to a doom that will not release it from in coils, West Europe has been wholly unable to meet, expect in a hand-to-mouth fashion, the insecurity of colonial poverty and obstruction that most threatens its existence. Out of fear and a kind of obsessed thinking, its conscious talk has been largely influenced by the internal conflict between capital and labour. In actual practice, however, and so far as vital consequences are concerned, the insecurity that has moved West-European capitalism in its entire being is the competition within its own ranks. Twice in the course of a generation it has sought to master this insecurity by wanting to reduce its members in war. The downward trend in productive capacity, world trade, and employment has been followed by the upward trend in arms industries and war.

Back of the two wars in this period, in so far as economic issues are involved, is the clash of productive capacities, the fact that the productive capacity of one capitalist structure cannot be fully used until that of another is laid low. This clash is over-laid by a number of cultural issues, and men might for all kinds of reasons ranging from narrow interests to democratic welfare, and even whole nations, get dragged into war as a measure of national freedom. All these reasons are perhaps important in the very long run; some are even economically important, and we will presently consider them in their bearing on West Europe. But both as to economic origin and consequences, the wars of this period are predominantly

21. At the peak of the 1929-33 depressions, nearly 10 per cent of the British and nearly 17 per cent of German populations were the unemployed and their dependents. At the time world trade also fell to about half its pre-depression size.

wars of productive capacities. The biggest economic dissimilarity in the two wars lies in the fact that the 1914 world war was almost wholly of West-European origin and making, while the 1939 war is only slightly more of a West-European character than it is of a Pacific set-up. Whatever else this might denote, it unmistakably shows that the spheres of economic vitality and arising disorders are shifting and that, comparatively speaking, West Europe is stepping back in history.

This stepping back is not occasioned by the destruction caused in the two wars. The direct destruction caused to a powerful country by war is seldom such that it cannot be made good by replacements. Rarely do the killings, however large they may be, outnumber the births, so that a war produces little effect on the numerical strength of West-European populations except with regard to the ratios between the age-groups. In like manner, the West-European productive capacity, whatever be the extent of destruction by land, sea and air, is continually renewed and even expanded in the midst of war, so that the end of a war finds a West-European power at a slightly higher productive level in certain directions than at the beginning. It is possible that the 1939 war, before it has ended, will have caused vast destruction; even so, unless they fight it out to the last factories, the productive capacity of West-European capitalisms will not have been appreciably reduced. Not war destruction but post-war incapacities reduce a people's strength. The morale of the peoples, however, is quite another question. There is no saying when a people might fade out of history as a result of repeated wars; the German example of a beaten people coming back soon to warlike vitality makes such calculations extremely hazardous. It might be said with caution that repeated and long wars may at some stage turn a people from the zest of this life to the bliss of the hereafter. Nevertheless, it is safe to treat the factor of people's morale as an unknown variable.

West Europe is stepping back in history as a result not of the destruction but of the shifts caused by war. The necessities of war cause such a disturbance in the ratios of productive capacities, and their use, of the world's Great Powers that continents and hemispheres gain and lose at each other's expense. The end of the 1939 war will probably have achieved a greater disturbance than the 1914 war did.[22] Impelled by the urge to eliminate the insecurity of each other's competition, West-European capitalism achieve through their wars of far greater measure of insecurity. The increasing insecurities of colonial poverty and obstruction, of competition from extra-

22. Of the world's seven Great Powers, at the beginning of the 1914 war, the ratio in favour of Europe was 5:2.

    Of the five European powers, the three West-European lands England, Germany and France, were, in view of their developed economies and productive capacities, genuinely Great Powers, while of the two East-European powers, Czarist Russia fell something short of a Great Power and the Austrian Empire was only nominally so. The end of the 1914 war saw no visible alteration in the world ratio, except that the nominally great role of Austria was taken up by Italy while Russia started making strides towards being a genuine Great Power. But back of this seeming stability in the world ratio a great change had taken place. The two extra-European powers, the U.S.A. and Japan, were so rapidly expanding their productive capacities and influence that one of them was preparing to be the world's greatest power while the other was amassing quite handsome chunks of power. At the beginning of the 1939 war, the ratio of world powers was nominally maintained, as before at 5:2 in favour of Europe, although real strength could best be measured by the ratio 3:2. The progress of the 1939 war has already seen Italy knocked down so badly that she may not again find it possible to strut about in peacetime as a Great Power in pretence. France is, in view of her defeat and for other reasons, unlikely to regain her productive or world-power position. Whatever may be the outcome of this war and whatever shifts may yet take place, Europe will have, with the most favourable ending, two Great Powers against two in the rest of the world. If Soviet Russia is to be one of these powers, her intervention in world affairs may continue in the political sphere, but is hardly likely, at least for sometime, to spread over to foreign trade and investments. That leaves just one Great Power for the whole of Europe whose productive capacity is relevant to the future of capitalism. Which ever this power may be, it will not only have defeated its other West-European competitors in war but will take care to see, at the end of the war, that not alone the military possibilities, but more so the industrial possibilities of its defeated foes are destroyed, or at least considerably curtailed. What this may mean

(*Contd. ...*)

European capitalism, and perhaps also of internal disorders are causing West-European capitalisms through their various wars to step back in the affairs of man.

The West-European population have lost their former rate of increase. Some are constant, while others have a very slow increase, and all are showing unmistakable tendencies towards great reduction by the end of the century. A reduction in population, however, does not necessarily imply a reduction

---

to Europe's share in world trade is not difficult to foresee. Although competing with each other, West-European capitalisms, in their clustering, were able to dominate world trade. Europe took over 51 per cent of world trade. The three West-European powers, England, Germany and France, took over 35 per cent of world trade. West Europe before the 1939 war was undoubtedly the economic centre and therefore also the military and political centre of the world. West Europe has irretrievably lost this position. This is so, not only because one West-European power has already lost its productive position and one more must follow suit, but also because the American hemisphere is coming up. The productive capacity of the U.S.A. has gone on expanding even in the midst of war, as illustrated by its fantastic aircraft production and Henry Kaiser's a-ship-a-day programme.

This expanded productive capacity is already manoeuvring for a corresponding position in the world's trade, air traffic, oil and other arrangements. Furthermore the U.S. economy has now used up its internal dynamic and must have recourse to an expanded world trade. The pre-war ratio in world trade between Europe and the Americas that stood at 51 per cent to 23 per cent in favour of Europe is likely in the post-war period to be reversed in America's favour, though perhaps not immediately to the same extent. At the same time the position of Asia in world economy might perhaps improve slightly. If Japan loses the war, the legacy of her productive capacity will to a considerable extent be taken over by China, and so, in any case, there will be one great power in Asia. A number of other economic and political movements are maturing whose course will to a large extent determine Asiatic development. The pre war share of Asia in world trade was around 14 per cent, and whether it greatly improves or not depends very much on extra-economic and unknown considerations. What these great continental drifts in world economy may mean to the future of capitalism will in some measure be considered elsewhere. Before we inquire into their significance, let us be aware of their existence. Suffice it to say here, therefore, the great continental drifts in world economy are taking place.

in its capacity to dominate over colonial economics or to wage war. What a population may lose in numbers, it may gain in technique. Actually, however, it is not so, in view of the fact that the technique of extra-European free economies is quite as advanced, if not more, and, furthermore, cultural and scientific stagnation does under capitalist conditions seem to go with a constant or declining population. The exact connection between cultural stagnation and a declining population is difficult to determine, except in so far as capitalism, because of a failing birth-rate, is denied a very vital internal dynamic, which, in a variety of ways, also causes it to lose its control over external dynamics.[23]

West-European inventiveness is also on the decline. With the rapidly increasing importance of electrical engineering and the internal combustion engine. West Europe is slipping back

23. West Europe nearly trebled itself during the 19th century, exclusive of the paupers who went to the U.S.A.; Britain quadrupled her population; Germany trebled herself; France more than doubled herself. These vast increase in population were helpful to West-European capitalisms in tiding over their industrial crises, as they offered enlarged markets and also supplied manpower for heavy capitalization. France's population has remained constant for over two decades now. The failure of Germany's deliberate effort to reverse population trends indicates that statistical calculations putting Britain's population at around 25 millions in place of the present 45 millions and Germany's at 35 millions by the end of the 20th century may not prove entirely unfounded. There seems to be great deal of truth in a British novelist's suggestion made about the imagined Forsyte family that the birthrate under capitalist conditions corresponds to the rate of interest. The falling rate of interest is threatening to become negative, and it seems hardly possible to check the accompanying decline in population. This reduction in population, however, does not by itself imply a reduction in West Europe's economic power against the colonial masses. As it is, in terms of the horse-power used, the German population is greatly in excess of India's and so is Britain's. Horsepower is a great determinant in existing forms of economic and political power. Nevertheless, one has to beware of the concentration of horsepower in the British or German style, for concentrated horsepower is a reason, among others, for population decline, and so forth. If the age that is passing belonged to concentrated horsepower, the age that is coming will belong to diffused, perhaps increased, horsepower.

from the unquestioned leadership in applied science which is held in the age of steam and steel. The German effort at substitute and synthetic industries is indeed a brave attempt at recovering by technique what is not naturally available; it is valuable for a closed economy but can hardly determine the world's economic career. It is more in the nature of a heroic effort to delay as far as possible West Europe's appointment with destiny.[24]

Colonial poverty and obstruction, more than any other factors, are forcing a contracting rigidity into the West-European economy. From Peking to Kahira and beyond, over Calcutta and Bombay, nationalism, at least with regard to consumption goods, is becoming the dominant spring of action. Except for some small and semi-fashionable sections of city-dwellers, the colonial masses show greater interest in where their goods are made than in questions of quality and price. Such an attitude is likely to grow and ramify with the passage of time, and its effect on the West-European economy can already be seen in the unlifting depression that has set upon Lancashire and Lyons. At the same time, colonial obstruction has been unable to produce any appreciable effect on West-European investments and production goods industries. With the exception of Mexico, where the British-

24. Whether the accoustic torpedoes, radio directed bombs etcetera, of West Europe's war machine are indicative of continuing scientific vigour or are the achievements of an old craft is difficult to tell. Perhaps Europe may yet take the lead in the sciences of small-unit horsepower and low-wattage electricity. As it is, the U.S.A. was already before the war the leading country in industries of electrical engineering, and the new science of electronics seems to be making great headway there. As the Asiatic countries are not burdened with the heavy capitalization of an old technique, there seems to be no reason why Asian scientists should not take the lead in the new sciences of dispersed techniques of electronics, plastics, and so forth. They have, however, not yet shown adequate scientific vigour and are dominated by the urge to ape European techniques of the industrial sciences. All this, however, should not in any way obscure the outstanding fact that West Europe is still the leader in the highest branch of science, that of mathematical physics.

owned Eagle Oil Company was confiscated, such attempts made elsewhere in this period, as for instance in Iran, have come to naught. Nor have any industries for the making of machines and machine-tools been set up in the colonies that may reduce the use of West-European capacity in production goods. While colonial obstruction, therefore, has great effect on West-European industries of consumers' goods, it has little appreciable effect on producers' goods industries.[25]

Much more than their deliberate obstruction, the increasing poverty of colonial masses is causing rigidity and contraction in the West-European economy. Through successive repetitions of the town-village relationship, over decades in some areas and over a century and more in certain others, colonial masses are no longer able to act as adequate life-givers to capitalist economies. They may yet delay West Europe's final stepping back in world affairs by their replacements of requirements for railways, public works, and consumers' goods industries, but these requirements are showing a tendency to contract. Unless prevailing economic trends are reversed, and that does not seem very likely, the increasing poverty of colonial masses will be the greatest single factor

25. A colonial population can determine the origin of consumer's goods even while it may be politically enslaved, but it cannot do that with regard to producers' goods, as the capitalization under existing technics is heavy and the market is almost entirely confined to a foreign government and native capitalists, so that it is influenced more by considerations of risks and prices and non-national interests than by national sentiment or interest. The repair and locomotive shops of India, for instance, have, in spite of 30 years' talk, remained assembly and repair shops, nor are they likely to become effective manufacturing centres for locomotives and automobiles. However, the economic movement in producers' goods industries begins when political movements have matured into success, and therefore this is hardly the place to predict how soon or how late colonial obstruction may start affecting the West-European industries in producers' goods. Incidentally, the Mexican confiscation with some compensation to American and British oil companies, although the result largely of Mexico's own national vigour, was partly facilitated by the attitude of certain influential interests in the U.S.A.

towards the undoing of the West-European economy.

Continental shifts in the use of productive capacity, tendencies to declining population and to loss of inventive vigour, and colonial poverty and obstruction are relegating the West-European economy to a back-seat in the affairs of men.

Let us now see if the purposive activity of West-Europeans is such as may stem their relegation to a back-seat. We will be concerned here with that aspect of purposive activity which produces tangible economic results; questions relating to motives, secondary aims, moral worth, errors, and of what ought to be done will be discussed when we take up the general problem of history.

The purposive activity of West-Europeans with regard to their greatest insecurity has tended, with the increase in colonial poverty and obstruction, to be more political than economic. This tendency is likely to grow, not so much because colonial obstruction will become increasingly active, but more so because the problems of colonial poverty are too baffling to admit of an economic solution by West-Europeans. Events no longer wait upon capitalist activity in the colonies, and it has very often to go counter to them, so that it is almost always left behind. West-European capitalisms are frightened of the development of cousin-capitalisms in the colonies, and they have even less vigour to work out a new system of technics that may bring wealth to the colonial masses and impetus to their own economies. Retention, not development, has become the colonial key action of West Europeans. With each repetition of the town-village relationship, the retainable volume will lessen, and West-European capitalisms will shrink with the shrinking of colonial economies.[26]

26. Recent West-European activity in the colonies has been of little economic consequence. The recent expenditure on canals, for instance, in Sind, Rajputana and the Punjab, although big in its own way, has in no way given a new dynamic either to Indian or to British economy. If there is any increased agricultural production, it is either just sufficient to cover the canal rates, that is, the interest and profits on government-owned canal

(*Contd. ...*)

West-European political activity in the colonies is simple. If colonial poverty is an insoluble problem, colonial obstruction is not quite that. By virtue of their political power, West-Europeans have to date been able to prevent a sudden cessation of the colonial dynamic through the revolutionary action of the colonial masses. They have also tried to appease colonial obstruction to the extent that is possible without danger to their own economies. When, therefore, West-European political activity in the colonies is not based on repression, it is informed by the tactics of investigating commissions, inquiry committees, reports, and piecemeal reforms. This is so not only when conservatives are in office, but also when popular front governments, such as those in France and Spain to which

---

capital, or it flows into the pockets of a very small section of big landowners without further productive use. At the same time, West-European activity in the colonies is assuming more and more a luxury character, as in, for instance, the Bombay Backbay Reclamation, the new Howrah Bridge, the Tanganyika Hunting Preserves, the Kenya Highlands, and so forth. These may make life more pleasant and beautiful for the west Europeans and a section of the native rich; they may even give a little retentive support to the West-European engineering industries; but they are absolutely powerless to revive capitalist or colonial economies. There is no likelihood of West-European economic activity acquiring a different character. Recent trends indicate that the West-European drift towards public works, transport, and what is now becoming known as agricultural mechanization will continue. Whatever their value as political or propagandist expedients, these measures of road-making, canal-making, electrified agriculture, and the like cannot revive colonial economies nor can they assist capitalist economies beyond making a small demand on the engineering industries. Until the internal relationships of colonial agriculture, among landless labour, poor peasantry, and big land-owners are radically altered and, what is more important, until colonial villages can undertake certain cooperative activities without much capital expenditure and can also reinvigorate themselves by some new type of small-unit technics, there is no hope for colonial economies. All this is beyond the reach of a foreign authority. There has indeed been some stray talk of a vigorous colonial policy, as, for instance, when a Secretary of the British Federation of Industries, speaking at a meeting of the Royal Institute of International Affairs, proposed the development of Africa and other colonies at a

(*Contd. ...*)

socialists and Marxian Communists were party, held office. Nor is this condition likely to change. The liberal conscience of West Europe, whatever its moral worth, is too uninformed economically to be able to direct the future of capitalism. Its solution to let the colonies develop themselves in freedom and to depend on their goodwill for such dynamic as they may choose to give has never been worked out in its economic details, and even if it were, there is no guarantee that it would prove acceptable to West-European governments.[27] Unless, therefore, some severe stress occurs as a result either of

---

negative rate of interest. In the first place, such talk is more an adventure in thought than a working policy, for West-European capitalisms will far sooner battle against the inevitable than accept such a vigorous policy full of grave and unknown risks; in the second place, it shows that even the most foresighted of West-European economists can only think of colonial development on the basis of old technics and therefore on the basis of diminishing capital. West-European capitalism, therefore, is likely to continue fighting a rearguard action on the colonial front; even more in the economic than in the political sphere must it forego all positive ideas and stick to the negative policy of non-liquidation. It can at best try to prevent the deterioration of the colonial dynamic to the extent that is possible by the employment of political methods. This will be so whether conservatives are in office or communists or any other variety between these two extremes. Marxism has no solution for the heavy capitalization of West-European industry. Its ready-made answer that, with the socialization of industry, everything will be all right, must appear strikingly irresponsible not only to the owners and managers of West-European industry but also to imperial labour with its subconscious insight into the need for colonial annexes. That is why Marxism has so far proved unacceptable to West-Europeans and their working class, and should it under some stress capture power it must, with its present understanding of the class struggle and technics stick to the economic policy of colonial non-liquidation or, else, if it chooses to fulfil its loosely held ideals, sent, the West-European economy hurtling along the path of relegation, of low production and unemployment.

27. Incidentally, this liberal conscience of freedom and justice is not to be confused with West-European communism. On account of its mistaken understanding of the world struggle, West-European communism, when it is not irritating its own nationals, is busy exasperating the colonial masses whose struggles it chooses to look upon as the expression of bourgeois and petite-bourgeois interests. It is thus ineffective and, to the extent that it befogs men's minds, somewhat harmful.

successful colonial obstruction or of great continental shifts in the ratios of productive capacity, West-European political activity in the colonies will continue to be based on the policy of retention. In the midst of shrinking economies, this political policy to retain whatever is possible can only mean the attempt to stabilize the colonial masses into the lowest caste of capitalism, much in the same manner in which Hindus of a disreputable period stabilized one of their own limbs into the caste of untouchables.

With regard to the insecurity presented by the clash of productive capacities, West-European purposive activity has been able to evolve nothing beyond international understandings of technical processes and certain quotas of production and trade. Such understandings, open or secret, are arrived at among the capitalists of deciding nations, and they have operated in spheres like oil, chemicals, and sugar. While they last, they are helpful in removing various sources of friction among different capitalisms but they are wholly unable to prevent war. As, however, West Europeans have no economic remedy other than this against war, there international understandings, when they are set up once again, are likely to cover extensive spheres such as foreign exchange and currency. They will undoubtedly help in delaying another outbreak of open hostilities among nations, not only because of the wide tie-up they will introduce among important national economies but more so because of lessened competition due to the post-war destruction of a few substantial economies. Nevertheless, these understandings can hardly prove enduring, as they will be strained, on the one hand, by the diminishing yield of colonial dynamic and, on the other, by the pressure of continental shifts on their stable systems of quotas of production and foreign trade. They can delay war, but they cannot prevent it. It is even possible that the war that comes after the operation of these very loose international agreements on production, currency, and trade may be genuinely deadly. Nevertheless, world capitalisms must pursue this policy of international understandings, for they have no other economic preventive against war.

The U.S. and Hindustan are graduating themselves into the two polarities of the rest of our world. If the U.S. has become the leader of the capitalist system, what happens there might yet deflect the sequel being worked out in West Europe; so has Hindustan become the chief arena for the shaping of an alternative economy.[28]

The U.S. productive capacity is higher than that of the three West-European lands, Germany, France and Britain, put together. Its productive capacity in mining and manufacturing, and that is what matters in the international relationships of world economy, is higher than that of the whole of Europe. But with this economic expansion the U.S. has fully exhausted its internal dynamic and used up such a dynamic as it could get from the other countries of the American hemisphere. There is now little question of further expansion; the U.S. is faced with the problem of preventing a setback into lower levels of production.[29] But the world is limited and imperialism is

---

28. The study of West-European economies has disclosed the main directions in which the capitalist system is developing among which is the shift in favour of the North American continent. We have now to find out if this shift alters or modifies any of the main directions. There is not much need, for our purposes, to study in detail the remaining major capitalism, that of Japan, as it is developing more or less along West-European lines, only that the caste-stratification is easier and the relegation slower. With respect to the two-thirds of the human race, the colonial adjunct of the capitalist system, our study of Hindustan will apply more or less to China, to practically the whole of Asia, to Africa, to the broad masses in the South and Central American Republics. Hindustan has become, so to say a mirror to these other economies. The chief among the colonial adjuncts has come to such a point of saturation that it reveals the many facets of colonial economy better than any other.
29. The enormous production of the U.S.A. as reflected in its yearly national income, which, with 'round Rs. 1,400 per head in a population of 13 crores, works out at one and three-fourths of the total in the three West-European lands, Britain, France and Germany, with an average of Rs. 750 per head in a population of 16 crores. It may be suggested that a higher cost of living and the greater range of services in the U.S.A. vitiate these figures and the

(*Contd. ...*)

territorially blocked. Increasing poverty in the colonies is causing a contraction in such capitalist economies as have so far been using them up. The leader of all capitalist economic will thus have to discover fairly soon whether it can enlarge an external dynamic in the process of using it to its own advantage. Is it at all possible to shunt world trade from its empire-colony rails to a new road which leads to expansion in the production equipment and consumption of all trading countries? The U.S. economy will have to tackle this question, not for its own good of the world, not for the good of the colonies, but for the own survival and for full use of its own productive capacity. If there is no answer to this question, U.S. capitalism must suffer the same tendencies to relegation and to transformation of class into caste which we detected in West-

---

productive capacity of the country should be assessed on firmer grounds. Of the world's entire primary produce in 1937, Europe shared 21 billion dollars, Europe including the U.S.S.R. shared 28 billion dollars, while North America, comprising, the U.S. and Canada, shared 15 billion dollars. These figures, however, do not give an adequate idea, as they are made up largely of food and other agricultural products. Confining ourselves to non-agricultural products, we find that Europe including Russia produced 39 per cent, Europe excluding Russia produced 30 per cent, while North America shared 40 per cent of the world's total. These non-agricultural products used in industry and manufacture give a true idea of the U.S. productive capacity, which is thus shown to outstrip that of the whole of Europe including Russia. That the Canadian productive capacity is here merged in that of the United States does not introduce a new factor, as it is comparatively small and is more or less an annexe of the U.S. Further evidence of the preponderance of U.S. productive capacity in the world economy can be had from certain figures of production in 1937; it may be remembered that this year was particularly favourable to Europe in view of its hectic rearmament.

	Europe minus Russia	*Europe plus Russia*	*North America*
Raw material	24%	34%	35%
Fuels and Power	30%	38%	47%
Metals	24%	36%	34%

(*Contd. ...*)

European capitalisms. We have therefore to find if there is any additional strength in U.S. capitalism which marks it off from its West-European cousins. Before we do so, let us broadly go over the entire scope of dangers to which we have found the world economy to be subject.

The severest danger to the world economy consists in the productive equipment of two-thirds of the human race. Denied the advantages of science and improving technics this equipment has been knuckling under the weight of foreign capitalisms, and labour done with its help is getting increasingly barren of yield. Five thousand crores of labour-hours under this equipment are of equal money-yield to 250 crore labour-hours in free capitalist economies. This great unbalance in the productive equipment of the human race goes

---

It is well known that the U.S. produced over 65 per cent of the world's petroleum in 1929, and has not allowed the ratio to fall very much lower; at one time it produced nearly 80 per cent of the world's automobiles; its production of steel and cotton was almost half of the world's. The 1939 war must have further expanded U.S. productive capacity; U.S.. leadership in the world economy must now be without parallel.

If U.S. productive capacity has on the one hand reached such amazing heights, it has on the other arrived at its peaks from where the downward passage is already showing. On the basis of 1929 being 100, the North American mining and manufacturing position had deteriorated to 93 in 1937 and 73 in 1938, automobiles had sunk to 89 and 46, while the index of producers' investment goods fell to 87 in 1937 and 54 in 1938. The U.S. has exhausted its internal dynamic. The expansion in railroads and allied industries, in internal roads and the automobile industry appears to have reached its limits; the 1929 production of 50 lakhs automobiles in a world total of 63 lakhs is an all-time record. Even the production of electricity can only be extended more with a view to tide over a depression than to satisfy real needs of expansion. There is also not much scope for expansion in the internal consumption of food or cloth. If may be remembered that the U.S. has used up whatever dynamic it could get from the South American Republics without going too far in the way of West-European empire-colony relationships.

What stares the U.S. in the face is that, despite almost ten years between 1929 and 1938 of increased population and scientific improvements, its

(*Contd. ...*)

with the equally great unbalance in its political and armed power. There are three major aspects of this unbalance. One aspect is whether the world's productive equipment at all its geographical points could be brought to the efficiency of yield that has been attained at any favoured point. If that were not possible, could the productive equipment of the retarded nations alternatively be so remodelled as to give an average per-worker yield of the world's production? These two aspects, however, relate essentially to the creative activity of the retarded peoples themselves, and the existing capitalisms can have nothing to do with them except in so far as to support the activity when necessary. But there is a third aspect with which the continuance of the existing capitalisms is bound up. This is the aspect of the decreasing yield of colonial labour-hours in a world where no new colonies can be annexed and those that have been are jockeying to get into their own. This decreasing yield of the retarded peoples is depressing the highly mechanized industries of the free economies. Time there was when this mechanization proceeded triumphantly

---

production-index of capital goods fell to 87 while that of Europe rose to 111. It would appear that the leader of capitalist economies is fated even more than the other members to suffer speedy contraction and relegation. When the 1939 war has ended, some of the West European capitalisms at any rate will have a lot of internal reconstruction to put through while the U.S. will have no such additional incentives in repairing war-destruction. There may be, a few years of animated demand in consumption and in the produce of limited new industries. The United States will thus be wholly unable to make use of its expanded productive capacity unless it chooses to utilize for post-war world trade the shifts caused in mid-war. Herein lies a reason for the decay of U.S. isolationism stronger than any articles of faith. The U.S. productive capacity demands involvement in world trade. It demands a world in which trade shall freely grow. Aside from the question of what a largely self-sufficient economy can exchange for its produce, the United States will have a still greater menace in the poverty and obstruction of two-thirds of the human race. If colonial poverty is primarily causing the relegation of West-European capitalism, it also remains to cause a lower use of the U.S. productive capacity. The most outstanding question, for capitalist survival, therefore, is whether the leader of capitalist economies will be able to face any better than West-European capitalisms the issue of colonial poverty.

with each new annexation, but the reverse process, going on all the time, has now become irresistible; larger and larger masses of men are getting thrown on the rubble of the outermost rings of the colonial circle. These men just do not exist either as market for foreign manufactures or as field of investment for foreign capital. To raise their consumption has always been a moral and a human need; it has now become an economic need of the free capitalist economies. This can only be done by improving the productive equipment of the retarded peoples and by so reshaping their internal distribution that larger masses may get a share at least of the increased production. We have found the West-European capitalisms wholly unable to face this issue of the productive and distributive equipment of the retarded peoples, and Japanese capitalism has also no solution except the short expedient of cheap-selling goods. The closed Russian economy is not yet concerned in an economic way with this world issue. It will now be our task to find out how far, if at all, the leading capitalism of the U.S.A. may give a new twist to this paramount issue of world economy and in what manner the retarded peoples themselves, as mirrored in Hindustan, may attempt to refashion their productive and distributive equipment.

Second only to this danger of retarded equipment in two-third of the world is the danger of prevailing technics. Heavy and large-unit technics have been the mode of a world in which application of science to industry is the exclusive privilege of a few powerful nations. These same technics cannot be spread throughout the world without being in some measure an act of simple displacement. If Hindustan and China are to build shipyards and make turbines and textile machinery of their own, they will no doubt add to their own wealth and in the process may add somewhat to the wealth of the world, but will also take away considerably from the productivity of the Japanese and British capitalisms that have so far supplied these needs for them. This, however, is a question which we may set down as insoluble in any foreseeable human future; no free nation would ever reduce its own wealth in order that another's might not be reduced nor would all the nations of the world agree to share equally in the fruits of human toil. Simple displacement in the application of prevailing technics to economy, and with it displacements in the wealth of nations are therefore bound to occur.

The more serious aspect of the danger of prevailing technics lies elsewhere. It consists in the unequal application of science and mass production to man's various demands. If it were possible to produce unlimited quantities of all types of goods, this danger would not exist. But that is impossible in any economy of any age or type. Even for such first demands as bread and milk, man has not yet found the means for their free municipal supply. Perhaps in a very intelligently managed economy under social ownership he may make of bread and milk free supplies like water, although in fixed equal quotas, but that too will take a very long time to come. The economy as a whole, whatever the ownership and management, must remain an economy of scarcity and price, unless a benevolent God gives us again a *Kamadhenu* or places us back in Adam's paradise. We cannot escape the price mechanism. In capitalist economies this price mechanism coupled with the needs of war has made for a block-use of science, not an all-round use. Science and mass production explore in any period a special bit of the territory of men's demands, this particular demand becomes most profitable to supply, and productive capacity in this sphere is pushed into great expansion. This is the basis of heavy mechanism, large-unit technics and mass production. The Soviet economy of Russia has indeed eliminated the profit motive, but has taken over the technical basis of capitalism, its block-use of science, its lop-sided large-unit technics. The problem of technics is therefore independent of the form of ownership in an economy and must be tackled separately. Otherwise it may make for specific industries, expanding and depressed by turn, for obstruction in changing over to better processes and materials, for foreign exploitation, for chimerical expansion, for concentrated destruction in time of war, and, above all, for hopeless mal-distribution of social understanding and intelligence and for an unequal distribution of wealth. An economy with large-unit technics and block-use of science cannot achieve balance.

This problem of technics is not to be confused with the demand to return to a simple life with few wants. Nor is it to be taken as an advocacy of simple spatial decentralization, now becoming quite a fashionable idea, in which all that is done is to break up prevailing technics into their several processes and to specialize these in different factories over different areas. It is as little to be taken for a denial of the machine or of mechanical and electrical power; it is not an advocacy of handicrafts. All these aspect are diversionary offshoots of the current problems of technics; the basic problem is not to cut down the use of mechanical or electrical power but to make it available for production in the same small units in the manner it is today available for consumption in prosperous economies as light, ventilation, or heating. This may increase the total wattage and horsepower in use; most certainly it would do so among the retarded peoples. This power would be a kind of maid-of-all-work, and there would be corresponding small-unit machines to process, not one bit of an article, but to produce the whole article. This will require almost a new beginning in science, a kind of flexible small-unit technics. It cannot be achieved at once, nor does it today seem at all possible in spheres such as those of turbine and automobile manufacture. But an economy must steadily aim to realize flexible technics wherever possible. Only so can an economy hope to achieve real and undepressing expansion and an equal distribution of wealth and social understanding. Only so can an economy acquire balance, in which man's various demands are orchestrated in a harmony of all-round application of science. So may perhaps culture and economy become joint partners in an enterprise of all-round and unhurried development in place of the order where culture is subject to an economy of piecemeal but fevered expansion. We have found privileged and imperialist West Europe burdened too much with its own past of heavy mechanization to take up flexible technics and Soviet Russia does not seem inclined to experiment with any new patterns of science. It will be our task now to find out if the U.S. has any contribution to make in this direction: more particularly, if the retarded peoples can summon up enough understanding and courage to show a new way of technics.

The third danger to world economy consist in private ownership and the corresponding forms of distribution. Critics of capitalism have fixed this danger in such well-known phrases as "the clash between forces of production and relations of production" or "the lag between production and purchasing power" or consumption. Even those who reject the theoretical scaffolding of these phrases, namely, the labour theory of value and the theory of surplus value, continue to talk of the main malady of capitalism as the clash between expansive production and contractive consumption. Actually, however, there is no reason why there would be contracting consumption even in a society where a considerable part of the annual wealth is usurped by the small class of capitalists and landowners. Such differentiation of consumption will take place that luxury goods play an unduly large part in the economy. The purchasing power of wage-earners and little men is restricted; not so of the owners, so that there will be a greater consumption of luxury goods and no necessary lag between production and consumption. It is, of course, possible that not all the earnings of capital are consumed and a large part of these are saved. These saving may be larger than what is possible to invest in further production. In such a case there will be a falling-off in consumption. But, then, this will be under-investment or the inability of production to expand. Actually, this is how the apologists of capitalism, with the reason or unreason of its traditional critics, are styling trade cycles and slumps. They maintain that during periods when an old demand exhausts itself, a scientific impulse runs out and no major inventions take place; production cannot absorb savings. In other words, the forces of production are weakened. What thus started as the theory of low purchasing power and contracting consumption in the hands of traditional critics of capitalism has now made its full circle as the theory of under-investment and weakened forces of production in the hands of its upholders. This is the fate of all theories which contain a partial truth. For a time they appear so true and brilliant, and then they are shown to be excessively wide-generalizations.

We know the origin of these errors and how wrong it is to think of production, consumption, and savings in abstract or as entities of an isolated capitalist economy. We have found them to be highly complex categories of a duality consisting of an inner capitalist circle and an outer colonial circle. The basis of capitalist development has lain in the clash between the expanding equipment of the free economies and the contracting equipment of the annexed economies, between imperial production and colonial production.[30] As such, the dangerous

30. We must continue to avoid all questions relating to the general theory of value. If in earlier parts of this study the term "value" has been used, it was more with a view to explain Marx's economic thought. And where the conception of surplus value has been attempted to be set right, it has stood for nothing else but the source and extent of exploitation that takes place in a world of political and armed inequality. One of the most prolific subject of economic enquiry is value and its measurement. But the results attained are hardly in keeping with the enormous labour spent on the subject. All the current theories of value are variations either of the labour theory or of the supply and demand theory. No formulation helps us to understand life's economic substance, for the formulation is rigid and eternal, while substance is fluid and historical. We have seen how Marx's socially necessary labour-hour as the measurement of value is all upside down in view of the imperial-colonial inequality in the application of science. The only thing really worthwhile in this theory is its ideal, its norms that the labour-hour should be enabled to produce approximately equally, whether in Timbuctoo or in Sydney, and that it should be given approximately equal consumption. In like manner, the supply and demand theory, also in its form of marginal units and preference-scales, deliberately ignores the forced conditions within which the narrow act of buying and selling takes place. This theory is perhaps good enough as a principle of accounting and industrial management, but as a mirror to value in changing economies based on changing forms of ownership and rule, it is hopelessly anaemic. All this discussion has perhaps proceeded from a question that does not exist; "What is value?" is like asking "What is God?" This may be a good

(*Contd. ...*)

consequences of capitalist ownership cannot be fixed in such abstract phrases as the clash between forces of production and forms of distribution. These dangers have to be viewed separately. The most important among these is the level of consumption among two-thirds of the human race. It is a consequence of the productive and distributive equipment of the retarded peoples, which is itself a consequence of capitalist rule over the world. We may merely note it here as one, the fact of colonial starvation, and two, the fact of blocked and falling consumption of quality goods of foreign manufacture.

When we confine our study to the distributive mechanism within the inner capitalist circle, most recent development discloses an increasing emphasis on luxury consumption in contrast to the consumption of necessities. In the measure that capitalist economies are unable to expand or even to make full use of their available productive capacity, there take place unemployment, seasonal employment, and price fluctuation that affect the wage-earners adversely. All this leads to underconsumption, both in quantity and quality, of the necessities of

---

enough question for metaphysics, but for economics the proper question relates to the price-mechanism through which a set of historical conditions translates itself into money-expressions. We must therefore avoid this discussion on value and retrieve from its debris the only article of value, that labour-hour, which, whatever its land, should be enabled to produce approximately equally and, whatever its form, should be assisted to consume approximately equally. For the rest, economics must study man as a producer under certain conditions and as a consumer under certain conditions. Our inquiry has related to the conditions of capitalist development. We have studied capitalism as a process in time. This has yielded certain results both as to the past and as to current tendencies that run into the future, but more so it is important as a method of inquiry. It may be possible, and perhaps worthwhile, to erect a logic of theoretical economics based on this method and the results, but that would be a vast and independent undertaking. Such a logic would presumably deal in detail with five entities: man in his economic dealings, productive equipment in its relative yield, world relationships, political rule, and economic ownership. Essentially these would be the two entities of labour and productive equipment, and they would act and react upon each other in the context of the three other entities.

food, clothing and housing; around-the-poverty-line consumption in the case of nearly 20 per cent of the West-European population. It is hardly likely that, so long as the profit structure and the world relationships of empire-colony production remain intact, any schemes of minimum wage and social security may offer an enduring solution of this vexing question. There is also a certain amount of voluntary foregoing of necessities in favour of fashion or entertainment, as in the case of the West-European girl who would deny herself a meal a day for a whole week so that she could get her dress laundered for the next ball. One can depend on capitalist civilization to keep up such expenditure. Essentially, however, the enormous earnings of capital in the highly-capitalized economies must partly spend themselves in luxury, as this is encouraged by lack of new fields of investment and by tax policies, and also because in its absence there would be a further fall in production and slumps would grow more acute. The structure of over-capitalized profits in the context of contracting economies turns luxury-expenditure almost into a kind of national virtue. There are, of course, various grades of luxury-expenditure, as of the low expenditure on necessities, but we may broadly describe this dangerous feature of capitalist distribution as the under-consumption of necessities and the growth of luxury-consumption.

But the distributive dangers of late capitalism go deeper than increased expenditure on luxury and blocked expenditure on necessities. The enormous earnings of late capitalism cannot be wholly reinvested or spent, and the larger part of these must perforce remain idle. It must be remembered that these earnings are the genii of a system by which the three West-European, U.S. and Japanese capitalisms meet almost wholly the world's demand in machine-tools, machines, transport, and power engines, and in a considerable range of manufactures. There is thus concentric force that pushes the world's capitalist profits into these centres. But there is now no pushing back of these as profit-yielding new investments or manufactures. We are already familiar with the main argument of this increasing exhaustion of the external dynamic, and we will yet have to straighten out some tangles; we will here confine ourselves to that aspect of the external dynamic which does not permit the reinvestment of its profits. Let us take one by one the fields of investment in the retarded economies. It would be highly dangerous undertaking to equip retarded economies with the industry of machine-tools, for, whatever the initial investment, Western capitalisms may thereby choke the way to their own sales of machines and engines. Except under irresistible competitive and political pressure from a stronger cousin, no capitalism can ever want to sell machine-tools where it can sell their products, locomotives, textile-machines, turbines, printing-presses, autos, dynamos and so forth. It would be the turning of an annual demand into a twenty-yearly demand, if even that.[31] Likewise, imperial capital, except of the U.S., has got so mixed up with the sale of manufactures to retarded economies that it would seriously depress itself if it chose to sell machines instead or invest in them; this danger has got fixed into the well-known phrase of the clash between Birmingham and Lancashire. Only such machines have been installed in the retarded countries as followed a long and bitter fight or as were not competitive with manufactures. Imperial capital would have preferred to sell electricity rather than turbines, if it could somehow, on cables or in any other way, ship the current with profit; it prefers to sell continually the electrical accessories of bulbs, radios, refrigerators, and the like to a limited clientele rather than risk supplying them with the machines to manufacture these. Along the entire gamut of machine-tools, machines, engines and manufactures there is an internal competition, and imperial capital therefore exerts its utmost to retain its areas of

31. In the year 1942, of around 1,000 per cent machine-tools expansion, the U.S. produced less than 2,000 million dollars worth of machine-tools against a total machine production 30 to 40 times as much. The U.S. machine-tools industry is likely to slump severely in the post-war period, for machine tools last 10 to 40 years.

consumer goods rather than seek investment in new fields of colonial production.

This rearguard and fear-stricken policy of retention is further encouraged by the fact that major capitalisms, including the U.S., have little capacity to absorb an increased produce from retarded economies. Their demand for food and raw material is not capable of great expansion, and such developments as increased food production in England and the U.S. quest in Arabia in pursuance of its oil-conservation policy are likely to cancel each other in their effects on world trade. Unless, therefore, the breath of freedom fructifies the science and technics of retarded economies so as to produce raw materials or quality goods, the problem of increasing their food and their primary produce remains an internal question, without effect on world trade. To increase the food and cloth supply of two-thirds of mankind may be man's greatest economic task, but world capitalism must remain indifferent to it as long as it offers no commodities for international exchange or return on investments. The colonial masses have interested imperial capital as low-wage producers of limited raw materials, as rate-payers on its transport and public utility installations, as consumers of its manufactures, and all this range of interest provides no scope for new investments. World capitalism has come to a dead end where new investments in the retarded economies threaten to choke off the source of its profits. The greatest distributive danger of late capitalism is thus the enormous accumulation of unproductive savings and the continued depression of the colonial equipment.

Aside from the distributive dangers, late capitalism continues the tradition of waste and deceit in production and, what is worse, deepens the element of chaos. As a principle we are already familiar with the industrial crises and trade cycles that are as old as capitalism itself, and we have also, traced how the territorial blocking of the external dynamic has thrown it into a condition of general crisis. But even in this condition there is no gradual decline, but general disorderliness and ups and downs. Unable to find new profits in the industries of life's staple substance, the methods of capitalist production lead themselves profitably to new industries of tenuous living on a mass scale. It is not for nothing that the industries that could still greatly expand in the decade before the 1939 war were those of films, radio, alcohol, and low-price fashions. Air travel and televised entertainment seem now to be on the list and, though various pep foods and vitamins might yet effect some improvement, the only staple demand that capitalism seems yet able to tackle and mass-produce is that of pre-fabricated houses. This will probably be capitalism's last useful contribution, not to the world, but to its favoured peoples. Capitalism goes where it finds profits, and this productive impulse must further exaggerate the importance of luxury-consumption, not alone of the high-income groups but also of the low-price mass-scale variety. In addition to this specific chaos of tenuous production, the general chaos of the regulation of an entire economy by the blind motive of profit remains. This motive expands the supply of certain demands beyond supportable dimensions, there is a scramble to contract just as there was a scramble to expand, and the sensitiveness of markets assisted by highly speculative expectations produces serious ups and downs.

A serious fall in the use of late-capitalism's productive capacity makes of war an almost irresistible temptation. When demand in producers' goods and transport falls very much below the supply arrangements, there is a temptation to shunt to war; if steel, autos, electrical equipment, and such like are not sufficiently purchasable for civilian use, their rate of consumption as tanks, jeeps, shots, and shells can be feverishly fast. The insecurity emanating from the unemployed millions disappears for a time, the victor hopes for enlarged exports to retarded peoples at the expense of the defeated capitalisms, and rationed consumption during the war serves to animate post-war civilian demand, just as it helps an imperial population to key up its war effort to a total pitch. If the index of producers' investment goods in a major capitalism is falling far too low, an experience to which late capitalism must be increasingly subject, and if it is elsewhere shooting up so high that armaments alone could have done this, the cunning of rulers has discovered no means other than war and its preparations as the way out. The greatest danger of late-capitalist production to world economy is its general and special chaos and its escape-mechanism in war.

It is surprising how late capitalism with its surfeit of savings and the comparative lack of new investment fields can still preserve a handsomely positive rate of profits. Should not capital flow into the available fields of investment and increase earnings or bring down prices and expand production, although in the process the rate of profit may fall so low that the rate of interest reaches the zero or the near-zero level? Against this natural development are operating the forces of monopoly, such monopoly as is the result of concentrated production as well as that which depends on the political rule of one country over another. The monopoly in production operates because of the huge amount of capital necessary to start rival and risky enterprises in the industries of producers' goods, because of government assistance, and of the national and international understandings of capitalists in the same industry. The monopoly in the foreign trade and investments of subject peoples can operate either nakedly or through the currency, tariff, purchase, and other policies through which an imperial government can easily shut out inconvenient competitors. These monopolies, arising out of imperial rule as also out of heavy mechanization, shut out rival capital, keep production low and prices high. Their aim is to maximize profits, while if they had not existed there would be expanding production, particularly among retarded peoples, at levels of nominal rate of interest. In fact, interest has about ceased its productive function in the major capitalisms. It still continues its distributive function of making the rich richer or of maintaining a *rentier* class. But its productive function is restricted to an expanding economy, when enterprises of old and new wants are continually added and interest serves as a regulator. In an over-capitalized economy that cannot further expand, interest is a dead weight and an obstruction to production. That the monopolies keep it up artificially prevents in particular the expansion of colonial equipment and does not allow late capitalism to face its distributive dangers. But such an artificial maintaining of interests bound to lead to a clash between capital that is being used and capital that is idle, capital that is tending towards extinction and capital that is artificially propped up to continue. This monopolistic maintaining of interest and profits as a productive factor in late-capitalist economies is thus a serious interference with normal development and the source and aggravation of the many dangers to which world economy is subjected.

The danger of private ownership in late capitalism may now be enumerated as, in the sphere of colonial economies,[32] the fact of starvation, the fact of falling consumption of foreign quality goods, the fact of enforced depression of the

32. The concepts, "retarded economies," "colonial economies," "outer circle," on the one hand and "major capitalisms," "imperial economies," "capitalist economies," on the other have been here used more or less synonymously. It might appear somewhat extravagant to lump together Hindustan, China, Iran, Sinhal, Misre, or the Congo under one category, in view of their varying political status. But on the deciding issue of capitalist development their status is similar, that of a retarded, colonial equipment which acts as an external dynamic to the major capitalisms. Without a doubt, there are two main economic camps in the world today and the basis of the division lies in the use of science and technics and in the yield and fruits of the labour-hour. Such an economy as that of South Africa is obviously colonial, with this difference that there is a very numerous middle class in the shape of the South African whites. The Australian economy, however, has slipped out of the colonial field, not because it is rapidly industrializing itself, but because the free application of science to its agriculture and sheep-rearing has enabled it to enter the world market with a raised status of the labour-hour. Nevertheless, it has certain mixed features, not the least important of which is its imperialistic exclusion of new settlers from a land almost twice as big as Hindustan with less than 1/40th of its population, and a corresponding dependence on a stronger capitalism, that used to be Britain but is now changing into the U.S.

productive equipment, and, in the sphere of developed economies, the fact of under-consumption of necessities, the fact of growth of luxury-consumption, the fact of unproductive savings, the fact of chaotic and war-making production, the fact of monopolist continuance of interest in an un-expansive economy. Some of these facts overlap each other and, in particular, the productive equipment of the retarded peoples. West Europe has been found to be wholly unable to overcome any of these dangers with the result that its classes are being transformed into castes and its economies are being relegated. By the abolition of private ownership, Russia has eliminated such of these dangers as have arisen in the inner circle of late capitalism but by virtue of being a self-sufficient closed economy has remained unconcerned with the outer circle of two-thirds of mankind. It will now be our task to find out how far the U.S. as the leader of late capitalism, and Hindustan, as the mirror and leader of the retarded economies, are likely to overcome these dangers in a constructive way.

Can the leader of late capitalism assist in reviving the productive equipment of the retarded peoples? In one essential it is differently placed from its West-European or Japanese cousins. While these have acquired a pervading interest in retarded economies so that they can sell their machines only at the expense of their manufacturers and their machine-tools at the expense of their machines, U.S. capitalism has no such burdensome past except to some extent in the American hemisphere. Its trade in manufactured goods with the retarded peoples of Asia and Africa does not play a vital role in its economy. It is free to sell them machines and machine-tools. It is thus unfettered enough to transact such trade and investments with the retarded economies as would increase the yield of their labour-hour. This introduces a new factor in the fortunes of capitalism. The prospect is opened out of restoring, perhaps temporarily, the imperial dynamic, which has ceased to expand with the enmeshing of the whole world and which has started contracting due to colonial poverty and obstruction. In making such sales and investments to retarded economies as they need and not as are forced on them by West-European and Japanese capitalisms, the U.S. economy can develop their productive capacity, can assist them in producing a very much larger volume of goods. There is thus a theoretical possibility that capitalism may yet be able to expand through re-equipping the colonial economies, where alone expansion is still possible.

Against this theoretical possibility must be set the peculiarly self-sufficient character of the U.S. economy, which distinguishes it from that of its West-European and Japanese cousins. The U.S. has much to give, but it can take very little. It is the leading producer in the world not only of producer's goods and manufacturers but also of food and raw materials. The other capitalisms are great consumers of food and processors of raw materials extracted from retarded economies; they thus maintain the gigantic town-village relationship between themselves and two-thirds of mankind. The U.S. economy has worked out this relationship largely within its own frontiers, beaten it into a kind of balance in the use of science, so that its great industrial production is matched by an equally great agricultural and mining production. The U.S. may be willing to sell machine-tools for the manufacture of locomotives of small dynamos, and also it may be wanting to increase its export in radios or fountain pens; in this quest it would want an expansive economy in the retarded areas, but what would it take in exchange? Not food crops, not fruit, not meat, not cotton, not iron, not petrol, no manufacture of mass-use, not any kind of the staple goods that are the bulk of world trade. The U.S. can give, but it cannot take; this hamstrings the leader of late capitalism in its effort to shunt world trade to the new rails of two-way expansion. If other capitalisms are unable to expand world economy for fear that this would hurt them, the leader of late capitalism may find that, while it had little to fear, its hopes were also ill-founded. It is, however, possible to exaggerate the inability of the U.S. economy to take, as it appears to us in the immediate present. With an expanding equipment in the retarded areas, the furs of Sinkiang, the skills of China, the brocades of Hindustan may come into such mass-use by the U.S. population as to become articles of bulk-trade.[33]

It is also possible that the retarded peoples, through their scientific ingenuity and collective effort, may yet produce new goods and raw materials to enliven world trade, but that can only come out of their free endeavour, and no outside agency can awaken it.

The leader of late capitalism would, in addition, be unable to use to the full its capacity to re-equip the retarded economies. To the U.S. has fallen the leadership of an economic system that has reached maturity, and as such it would be unable to interfere too much with the existing arrangements. The West-European capitalisms, ably supported and rivalled by the Japanese, have knit up the larger part of the retarded world into a political rule that guarantees the working out of the town-village relationship. The U.S. must accept these different imperialisms as so many agents of stability, and when it is not at war with one or the other it must work in collaboration with them. There may be an

33. It wouldn't be such a fanciful thing if the U.S. handed out scrips to its citizens for travel and stay in those areas from which it would not otherwise receive payment. Such travelships could be granted on the close of secondary studies or marriage or some such general occasion applying to all citizens, and the internal arrangements between the U.S. government and the investors and exporters would not be impossible to make. It is, however, doubtful if even the U.S. could summon up sufficient courage to do this for the mass of its citizens. Likelier it is that the U.S. would want to become monopolist, the collector of old treasures and the user of new luxuries of the wide world. That travelships or treasures would raise the U.S. so infamously above the rest of the world in luxury and in what is known as culture is a moral fact with which we are not here concerned. But, while we may think out all the possible ways in which U.S. could receive payment from other economies, let us not forget that the debts and reparations owed by post-1919 Europe were defaulted, partly because Britain and Germany were not over-particular about their credit, but more so because the U.S. had no use for their manufactures or raw materials.

under-current of hostile competition, there may at times be bitter clashes and wars may not always be avoidable, but, as a general measure, the U.S. must accept these imperialisms as stabilizing agents in an otherwise uncertain and unforeseeable world. The retarded peoples themselves may hold quite another view of what would really constitute a stable world, but the leader of late capitalism would need incalculable courage to experiment with a stability that is yet to emerge. Calculably, therefore, the U.S. would have to compromise with imperialistic trade policies, and its supply of producers' goods to retarded economies would be limited. In addition, U.S. capitalists would prefer to transact their sales and investments with groups of capitalists among the retarded peoples, rather than encourage a socialist reconstruction. Although this is a question which we will yet examine in greater detail, it is extremely doubtful if the re-equipping of retarded economies can be carried out by their capitalist classes.

But the U.S. economy will be forced, to whatever extent it can, to expand its dealings with retarded economies. Its state of continued slump will force it to do so. It cannot continue on a basis which compelled its index of producers' goods to fall from 100 in 1927 to 87 in 1937 and 54 in 1938, and certain intervening years were worse, while that of Britain rose to 133 in 1937 and 199 in 1938. Not all of America's fall or Britain's rise could be explained by the arms industries; a considerable part of it was due to the same condition which made the rate of industrial profits in the U.S. fall from 12.8 per cent in 1929 to 2 per cent in 1932, 6.7 per cent in 1937 and 3.8 per cent in 1938, while that in Britain was maintained at the comparatively steady levels of 10.5 per cent, 8.5 per cent, 11.2 per cent and 12 per cent in the same years. It is significant that the majority of U.S. manufacturing companies registered negative rates of profit for the years 1931 and 1932. The U.S. cannot fail to notice that Britain is able to steady its fall by the use of the external dynamic, which, although deteriorating, is still capable of providing replacement orders and limited quality consumption. The U.S. economy, however, has completely exhausted its internal dynamic and also such as it could get from the American hemisphere, with the result that if it is to save itself it must hit out for an external dynamic, which may be enlarged while being used. Recent developments are arousing a kind of vigour, albeit naive, that aspires to cope with this task.[34]

---

34. Let us first acquaint ourselves with the vast increase in U.S. productive capacity that has taken place as a result of the war. A Federal Reserve Board index places industrial production in 1943 at 2.4 times the average of 1935-39. It is thus roughly three-quarters over again of the 1929 production. Less than 30 per cent of this production is for civilian use, while the rest is war goods, which have gone to different parts of the world. What will happen to this enormous productive capacity when it is reconverted to peace use? It will naturally burst to make use of the world routes that it discovered in war.

    Quite surprising are the opinions expressed by U.S. businessmen, chief among whom is the President of the U.S. Chamber of Commerce. He is reported to have said sometime in 1944 that the only way to achieve an expansionist economy in the U.S. is to supply producers' goods, capital and skill to the backward economies. Without awareness of the basis of capitalist development, the U.S. Chamber President has, through sheer electric observation, come to a conclusion to which our analysis of capitalism has brought us. Mr. Eric Johnston also talked to the British people in October, 1943 on the function of capital: "In its British-American intermingling, it shall include an intermingling with whatever capital may volunteer itself in the regions of new investments. And, finally, it will not recoil but rejoice on the day when every such region stands up alive and alert on its own business feet." In the course of a revealing conversation with the chairman of the British Imperial Chemicals, who thought that American anti-monopoly legislation stood in the way of a wide Anglo-American international understanding, Mr. Johnston maintained that American capital still believed in individualism and competition and that even a concern like the General Motors could not depend on state action to pull it through in peacetime. British capital is too wise to be able to rejoice; American capital is too innocently robust to recoil. We are not here concerned with who is right, whether or not the prospect of a producers' goods industry in Hindustan or China should frighten the Americans as much as it already frightens the British. And we have already indicated the severe limitations upon any American attempt to develop backward

(Contd. ...)

With regard to the productive equipment of retarded peoples, we may now sum up the U.S. position as the absolute need for an enlarging external dynamic and the willingness to supply producers' goods on the one hand and, on the other, the necessity to collaborate with existing imperialisms for being agents of stability and the comparative inability to receive a large volume of goods from other economies. It is easy to see that this is an exceedingly divided position. The only positive results that may be expected from it are some displacements of the existing volume of world trade[35] and some expansion of the retarded economy of China such as is not politically enslaved. The pressure of the U.S. econ-

---

economies, which are likely to turn it into more talk than activity. The robustness, nevertheless, stands out with which Americans are trying to grasp that the only way to achieve an expansionist world economy is to supply producers' goods to the retarded economies.

In this connection, it would be worthwhile to disabuse our minds of the complex issues raised to elaborate the American attitude towards retarded peoples. Much is made of the Declaration of Independence and the articles of the Constitution or even of the American's inability to wear a dinner jacket while dining alone in the tropics, and these spiritual and psychological traits are adduced to prove that U.S. citizens are opposed to imperialism. It is not yet our scope to examine the values of spiritual and psychological qualities in human affairs, although we may be permitted to doubt how far such qualities can withstand the pressure of other forces in international dealings. It is with these other forces, in so far as they are economic, that we are here concerned. Incidentally, the Russian economy enjoys a position similar to that of the American, in so far as neither has acquired such a vested interest in the consumption of retarded peoples as to be unable to supply them with producers' goods. The difference comes in where the Americans are forced in their own interest to exploit their position, while the Russians have yet a lot to do with their internal expansion.

35. In an earlier chapter, we have seen how the war is causing shifts in world trade and productive capacities and how this, combined with other factors, is causing the relegation of the West-European economy. There seems hardly a doubt that the U.S. will try to make full use of these shifts for its post-war economy; its world shipping, air traffic, trade in machines and goods, foreign investments are bound to grow at the expense of the West-

(*Contd. ...*)

omy may also compel its capitalist-imperialist cousins to permit or undertake a very limited expansion of the colonial equipment. For the rest, the U.S. will play a pervadingly obstructive rule. If it will obstruct the West-European and Japanese capitalisms in stabilizing the colonial peoples as the untouchables of the capitalist system, it will also obstruct the retarded peoples in availing themselves of such opportunities as make for a sharp break with the past. That it will thereby be unable to prevent successive fall in the use of its own productive capacity or genuinely expand the productive equipment of the retarded peoples can be said without hesitation. It will not have provided a positive dissipation of the severest danger to world economy. How long it will be able to delay the hardening of declining capitalism into a worldwide caste structure or the advent of a wholly liberated world economy is another question. The world index of production and its tendencies would show that either the one or the other must happen well before our century is out. Capitalism must either harden into a world-hierarchy of castes or it must be blown up with the advent of liberated economies, and the U.S. will meanwhile obstruct either solution and be generally negative. In its most recent development with regard to retarded equipment the U.S. economy is showing a tendency to divided interests and delaying action. The leader of late capitalism has thus already about relinquished its leadership of the colonial peoples; will they submit by becoming increasingly starved helots of a declining capitalism or will they rise into manhood?

The technical danger in the U.S. can be assessed from the fact that, while the index of total production fell from 100 in

---

European economies. At the same time, this growth will be unequal to the needs of the American economy, so that, in spite of the continental shifts in favour of the U.S., the major fact of colonial poverty and obstruction in conjunction with the heavy mechanization of capitalist economies will be there to cause the relegation of the U.S economy. That the process of this relegation will be different and will produce different consequences has already been indicated.

1929 to 73 in 1938, the output per man-hour rose from 100 in the earlier to 116 in the later year. Scientific and organizational improvements are continually increasing the yield of the labour-hour, but there cannot obviously be a corresponding and unceasing increase in the production of known goods. The hours of work must therefore be reduced or men thrown out of work and it is usually the second alternative which materializes. The shock of continuous improvement in the known lines of heavy mechanization and mass-produced goods can only be observed if scientific vigour can at the same time create new mass-wants and the means to satisfy them. Aside from the question of whether each continuous expansion of wants is desirable, the U.S. experience shows that it is no longer possible. The great new line of which much is being made today is air traffic. According to a U.S. statement, the aircraft industry and traffic personnel would in coming years give work to anywhere between 6 per cent and 10 per cent of the entire population. This appears a highly inflated estimate, but, were it true, it could only be effected largely at the expense of rail and ship traffic. As such, it would not be the creation of a wholly new work. Although scientific vigour is abundantly improving known lines and synthetics, there is not adequate evidence that U.S. economy could match it by hitting out into wholly new venues. This will cause a forced depression in technical progress from one industry to another; there will be no unhurried and balanced use of science, and stability will not come.

U.S. science is, however, not oblivious to the problem of flexible and small-unit technics. The war has, for instance, given it the jeep. This is a kind of maid-of-all-work; it can plough the fields, furnish power for milking, in addition to being an auto. The U.S. Department of Agriculture has calculated that the jeep can do the job of a heavy tractor with the petrol consumption of a half gallon to the acre, in place of the tractor's 3.3 gallons. There can be no better illustration than the jeep of the new technics that we must strive for; all-purpose, small capitalization, low running expenses. In like manner, U.S. exporters are reported to be busy perfecting small dynamos for use in retarded economies, which would cost 15 dollars to the horsepower in place of the former 40 dollars. All these experiments in small-unit technics are, indeed, offshoots of an economy that promises to remain predominantly large-scale and heavily mechanized. The U.S. can no more make a sharp break with traditional technics that West Europe can. Nevertheless, these experiments and others being made on the uses of low-watt units may inspire retarded economies to base their industrial renovation on a purposeful striving after small-unit technics.

The U.S. science will yet add to the amenities of life; it will give gas that heats and also cools; it will give new materials like plastics and new fibres to wear, new drugs and surgery, and, of course, new weapons of war when needed, and on the whole it will make life more comfortable, at least for the majority of its citizens. But, beyond grazing the problem of small-unit technics and thus maturing it slightly, U.S. science will not have provided a new technical base that can sustain a more purposeful production, distribution, and defence.

While West European pursues the policy of international understandings among capitalists without much talk and beyond the common gaze, the most talked-about anti-war measures are the abrogation of national sovereignty, the pursuit of disarmament or limited arms, and the establishment of a world league and a world police. One does not have to refer to their history in the past to be able to predict their ineffectiveness in the future. They go wholly counter to the existing economy based on imperial-colonial division of labour and on multiplying capitalisms within a territorially blocked imperialism. As such, these measures will remain barren of action so long as some great spurt of economic thinking does not concretely link up world justice with national welfare or the contending capitalisms do not reach a stage of utter inaction. Until then they will remain moral precepts, awakening, at best, a vague hope for the future and a vaguer attitude of criticism towards the present. Much the same thing can be said of the concept of class struggle preached by West-European Marxists as a preventive of war. Twice has it failed, once in the case of the Second International and again in that of the Third International, to turn an imperialist war into civil war, and thus into peace. This cannot be otherwise, for the West-European class struggle between capital and labour is cut across by the more deciding and worldwide empire-colony relationships and their results, the competing capitalisms. Until colonial economies can fully succeed in their obstruction, the Marxist concept of class struggle can, at best, act as a negative influence on West-European policies, a hamper and a source of confusion.

In respect to the insecurity of war, the effective activity of West Europe is thus the pursuit of international economic understandings and the preparedness for war. In fact, a deepening of this second aim goes noticeably with the steady deterioration of West-European capitalism; the earlier aim to be able to wage war when it comes is being replaced by the newer aim to keep ever prepared for war. This need of preparedness for war can best be met by the institution of a stable military caste. Unless prevented by forces outside itself, West Europe is heading towards such an institution.[36]

West Europe's purposive activity in respect of internal capital-labour relationships has shown an outward variety.

---

36. Should it be possible to destroy the productive capacity of any of the free capitalist structures after the 1939 war has ended, there will be need to hold these in subjection, and consequently the need for war-preparedness will grow. A kind of officers' caste already exists in West Europe. All that is needed is to broad-base it. How exactly this will be done or whether it can be done at all will depend on several factors outside of West Europe. Incidentally, the introduction of a caste system seems to be done only as a palliative against the declining birthrate in a capitalist economy. What capitalism with its falling rate of interest does to the numbers of a population can only be undone by religion and the absence of any recreation save that of producing children. Such an increase of population may in the earlier stages act as a dynamic force, but that it will, in later stages, fall a

(*Contd. …*)

Among other items, state action intended to ensure wider education, health schemes, unemployment and pension benefits has grown in recent times. We are not at present concerned with the importance of such state action to the habits of a people or to their way of thinking. But its economic significance can, for instance, be grasped from the calculations of British economists who have estimated the redistribution of their national income from the rich to the poor caused by such state expenditure at around three per cent. While the attempt to extend such state action bring obvious benefits in other spheres, it must be understood that the little extension[37] that may still be possible can in no way alter the basic capitalist character of the West-European economy.

Some efforts towards social enterprise like the Municipal London Transport or the Berlin workers' house have attracted considerable attention. The relevance of such socialization to the capitalist system is more controversial than real, for the economy as a whole is not affected by it. Immense sectors of the economy, almost the whole of it, continue to remain in capitalist hands as a result of such scrappy socialization. Further, while the bringing of London Transport under municipal ownership held public attention for a number of years, capitalist enterprise was meanwhile busy recovering many times larger sectors through its enlarged industries in automobiles, radio engineering, and aeroplanes. Socialization is scrappy unless it affects a majority of sector in a capitalist

---

victim to the cultural and even military sloth that a caste system causes should not be disputed. Also, a caste system with a good birth-rate cannot exist without child labour. West Europe will have to devise some means whereby its once-payable bonus to fertile parents may be turned into a recurrent income.

37. The small scope for extension may be seen from their government's opposition to the Beveridge Scheme for the people of Britain. It has been calculated that the cost of this scheme would not be more than that incurred in the destruction of Hamburg. This expenditure would no doubt be recurrent, but has not the war as a whole already cost hundreds of times as much? Again, the very minor expenditure on the destruction of rats in the London sewage system could only be thought of in wartime.

economy and unless, while a single municipal or state-action is raising the heat to controversy, care is taken to prevent the springing up of great new sectors of capitalist enterprise. Present trends indicate that attempts at socialization in the West-European economy will continue to be scrappy and leave its capitalist base unaltered.

The movement to associate the working class with the management of industry gathered some force under the Weimar Constitution in Germany, but even during its brief existence it did not show much promise of causing any great change. Workers' councils can at best check deterioration in wages and conditions of work; for the rest, they persuade the working class to acquire similar perspective on foreign trade as those of the managers of industry. It is indeed surprising that West-European capitalists have not chosen to associate their working class with the management of industry; this may partly be due to the conflict between a rising or fixed wage and a shrinking economy, but it is also due to irrational class-prejudice.

We may now consider if the independent class action of West-European workers has fared any better than state action of various types in solving the internal conflict between capital and labour. The outstanding fact may first be noted that working class action in the three deciding West-European capitalisms has at one time or another been brought face to face with the possibility of a structural change in economy. There was a revolution in Germany, and the barest avoidance of another; there was a general strike in England; there was a Popular Front of progressive parties in France. But nowhere could the West-European working class seize such political power as to end capitalism. No doubt it was considerably hampered by the attitude of the numerically powerful middle classes of the West-European economy, which derive a substantial part of their income from the imperial-colonial division of labour. Could not also be that the West-European working class itself stood paralyzed in its action because of this international division of labour? What has been described as its betrayal by its leaders is perhaps to some extent the awesomeness with which the West-European working class has beheld its heavily capitalized industries whenever it has come within an ace of political power. The dread that the whole structure might crumble to pieces in its hands has held it back. It could not, as in Russia, be the creator of a new development; it could only be the heir to a very heavy old development that depends on the rule over colonial masses. It has not unnaturally been steadily retreating from all ideals of a revolution or a general strike to capture power. Until West-Europeans can be made to see some new economic way that links up their national welfare with the destruction of imperialism, this retreat of the working class seems to be as unavoidable as the relegation and other phenomena of the West-European economy that we have hitherto noticed.

But the partial struggles and strikes of the working class have made a great difference to the most recent development of capitalism. They have made difficult the passage of West-European society from a class structure to a caste structure. It is not as if West-European workers are averse to stabilizing the class-structure of their economy; what they have fought to achieve in their struggles for wages and a closed shop is a point of stability favourable to them. But the capitalists of the shrinking economy of West Europe have also been seeking for a point of stability most favourable to them. Herein lies the clash, and not in any dynamic struggle of larger objectives. At what point shall the classes be transformed into castes? West- European purposive activity has shown a duality in that point favourable to labour and unfavourable to capital.

The West-European tendency toward the transformation of classes into castes can be seen clearly in the Nazi movement of Germany. All kinds of internal mobility in the economic structure of Germany are stopped by the use of political power. Labour get wages fixed by the state, it moves from one place of work to another at the dictate of the state, its conditions of work and leisure and its corporate activities are determined by the state; in like manner, the state fixes the profits on capital, new investments are directed by the state, and the state determines the order in which different industries shall get priorities on capital, raw materials and labour. To assert that this immobile arrangement has been generally irksome either to capital or to labour is to close one's eyes to the big fact that the demand for security in the West-European economy is rapidly ousting whatever demands there formerly were for great changes of system. Further, this internally immobile economic structure openly recognizes the need for external dynamic, the need, therefore, to stabilize the colonial masses of Eastern Europe and elsewhere into the untouchables of capitalism, and thus gives a united perspective to the entire people, whereas in other West-European countries this perspective is consciously held alone by the ruling classes and the working class is only dimly aware of it. In this manner, German economy has taken a big step towards the transformation of classes into castes, when other West-European economies are fumbling towards it.

Even in England, a miner's son is generally a miner's father, and a similar condition would obtain with a spinner or a smelter. Migrations of individuals from one class to another do indeed take place with greater ease than would be possible in a caste system, but what distinguishes a class structure from a caste structure is the economic movement of the class as a whole. A class is a group that moves economically; it aspires to better its position. A caste is a fixed economic entity; its aspirations lie in some kind of a debased religion and the doing of certain hierarchical duties. There is hardly a doubt that the most recent fight of the West-European working class for a minimum wage, collective bargaining, the closed shop is no longer an attempt to move economically but is an effort to get fixed as a comparatively favoured caste of capitalism. On the other hand, capitalists wish to fix the working class at a point low enough to ensure their own privileged position in the midst of a shrinking economy. A great drama of caste stratification is being played out in West Europe; the contestants themselves are often unaware of the significance of their roles; and it is doubtful if there will be a coherent ending at all. The contestants may break each other with their inability to find commonly agreeable points of stability. The liberal and Protestant ethic may prove too tough to be given a new slant. Some great new activity of conscious social change cannot be entirely ruled out. The colonial masses will probably refuse to be treated as the lowest caste of capitalism. It is also possible that the theatre of this drama will continually slide back into the backwaters of men's affairs so as to lose its exciting interest. Whatever may happen, the deciding effect of West Europe's purposive activity, no matter what the motives of men are, is to create a big movement for the transformation of classes into castes. That this movement, when it has fully matured, must mean cultural death is here irrelevant.[38]

---

38. Already, a blight has settled on West-European thought, in particular on its various sociological sciences. In fact, it is doubtful if, outside of the Dionysian clash of arms and the presentation of drama, there is anything great still left in the West-Europe. The economic man is ending, not to be replaced by a healthier faith or ideals, but in utter despair, as he is no longer able to rule over the world. West-European philosophy, sociology, economics, politics, literature are going scholastic and are increasingly concerning themselves with marginal phenomena. However, the proper place to discuss the cultural relegation of Europe would be when we take up the general problem of history. We may here confine ourselves to economic thought by way of illustration. In the two most important West-European countries, economic thought has proceeded along revealing lines: in Germany, it has become photostatically historical and has lost the creative urge; in England, its discussion of economic phenomena is proceeding in an increasingly rarer air.

    The German Werner Sombart, perhaps the greatest West-European economist of the century, has cutely described the current economic movement as tending towards social pluralism. Incidentally, this social pluralism in economy is not to be confused with the philosophical pluralism in thought. It only means a kind of balanced economy in which industry, handicrafts, agriculture, the captains of industry and its workers all have their fixed places, duties, and rewards. So far, this is a correct

From this rapid survey of recent capitalist development, we find two major tendencies to the relegation of the West-European economy and to the transformation of classes into castes, and also some ineffectual attempts at conscious social change. The two tendencies are not inimical to each other, and unless one or the other of the stresses already indicated awakens a new thinking and activity, the West-European

---

historical observation; we have already seen how the West-European economy is attempting to achieve fixity and caste. But, when Sombart goes on to add that this economy of social pluralism will by itself endure in a state of prosperity, he is unhistorical, and therefore uncreative. His unhistoricity proceeds from his unawareness of the deteriorating colonial dynamic and of the continental shifts; his lack of creative solutions is also to be ascribed to this unawareness. Nevertheless, Sombart will enable the student of the future to understand a part of the world of today and its aspirations.

British economist, statisticians excluded, are, on the other hand, discussing phenomena of money, interest, wages more or less in scholastic way and with a view to refine their definitions. Thus one of these, Mr. T.R. Hicks, pleads, in respect to consumers' demand, for a change from the method of "total utility" to "scales of preference," from "marginal utility" to "marginal rate of substitution" among preferences, from "diminishing marginal utility" to "diminishing marginal rate of substitution". These newer terms indeed make better sense than the old categories. Precision should always be welcome, but there is just a possibility that in the search for it economics might be turning into grammar. Mr. Hicks goes on to describe the conditions of equilibrium in a dynamic production plan: "(1) The marginal rate of substitution between outputs of any two dates must equal the ratio of their discounted prices; (2) the marginal rate of substitution between inputs of any two dates must equal the ratio of their discounted prices. (3) The marginal rate of transformation of any input into any output must equal the ratio of their discounted prices." Mr. J.M. Keynes's definition that "Short-period supply price is the sum of marginal factor cost and marginal user cost" is on a par with this. All this is *Panini* with a vengeance, without his brevity and without the easy-to-remember rhythm of the language whose grammar he refined. Precise simplicity is something entirely different from complex precision. The crux of the complex writing just quoted is that calculations of future costs and prices, or income should be so made that the interest payable during the period is deducted from them, and that a production plan must take account of the

(*Contd. ...*)

economy is fated to slide back with the attempt of its capitalism to stabilize and stratify.[39]

Russia broke away from the capitalist system nearly three decades back, and on the surface her development should have little to tell us about the working of capitalism. However, a study of her development will indicate not only possible ways in which it has affected capitalism adversely but also

---

most profitable substitutions between present output and future output, between present input and future output. Innocently unaware of the political and historical world in which their economic phenomena move, British economists have in recent years discussed the problems of money and interest in such isolation as to give them a kind of self-movement. This is not to say that their findings are all useless. Mr. Hick's definitions, for instance, of the simple term "income," though to some extent delightfully virtuous, are penetrating and should persuade the creative economist and the economic historian to be wary of certain pitfalls. Is income, "the maximum amount which can be spent during a period if there is to be an expectation of maintaining intact the capital value of prospective receipts"? No. Is income then "the maximum amount the individual can spend this week, and still expect to be able to spend the same amount in each ensuing week"? No. Is income "the maximum amount of money the individual can spend this week, and still expect to be able to spend the same amount in real terms in each ensuing week"? No. Income is what a person "can consume during the week and still expect to be as well off at the end of the week as he was at the beginning." The week is only a convenient period, and it may be noted that the first definition is incorrect in view of changing rates of interests, the second in view of changing prices, the third because it is concerned with expenditure and not with consumption, while the fourth, although correct, is indeterminate. Such is British economic thought today, not creative, not historical, not even logically simple, but perhaps negatively helpful.

39. In Marxian language, the study of the West-European economy discloses three laws in operation: the law of relegation, the law of transformation of classes into castes, and the law of conscious social change. The first two laws are prevailing over the third, and will in all likelihood continue doing so. The Marxian law of class struggle, which is a rather misshapen effort at social change, embraces only a small part of world realities. In attempting to raise this bit to the status of a whole, Marxians are to some extent strengthening their class enemies. The communist illusion that the world has already been mapped out by the Marxian laws of capitalist

(*Contd. ...*)

whatever capitalist traits it has carried within itself. A major difficulty is the lack of verified information on certain aspects of Russian economy. Even more so is it difficult to separate the essential from the marginal in a still considerably fluid economy.

Russian economy has pursued two objectives: to socialize and to modernize. In both these aims it has been guided essentially by Marxist theory. With regard to the objective of socialization, the initial step was economic, the establishment of social ownership and control over the means of production, while the rest has been left to political action, the liquidating of capitalist remnants or what are known as the counter-revolutionary elements. In pursuit of the objective of modernization Russian development has been given the definite character of large-scale production, of heavy capitalization. By "modern," Russians have naturally enough understood the latest stage of capitalist production, which, in Marx's view of history, is also the highest, since out of it was to have arisen the socialist society, and which, within the capitalist world, has established its superiority in war as in peace. This is monopoly production, mass production, and Russians have apparently taken for granted that the economics and advantages of large-scale production, which place one capitalist firm in a preferential position over another, must also apply to a nation's economy as a whole. Out of this belief and the objective to modernize, the Russian economy has closely followed the latest capitalist techniques

---

development, that socialism is an inevitable outcome of highly capitalized economies, and that all there is to do is to evolve a ruthless will is causing considerable harm. Socialism requires a great new effort at renewed understanding of capitalism as much as it requires an effort of will. To believe that the task of understanding was completed by Marx is the gravest communist error. Unless the West-European peoples, in particular their working classes, can work out their class struggle in subsidiary alliance with the struggle of the colonial masses and unless they review the problem of technics in its world-character of an equal attack on poverty, they are heading towards a relapse.

of large-scale production and has thus produced certain traits which bear a family likeness to capitalism. How far this likeness is superficial and in what measure, if at all, the objective to socialize clashes with the objective to modernize is the intriguing question that comes out of Russia. For the present, let us grasp that the Russian economy has pursued the two distinct objectives to socialize and to modernize in a large-scale way.

The Russian five-year plans have in consequence been weighted excessively on the side of large-scale industries, of producers' goods, and of mechanized transport. Consumers' goods have been produced to a minimum extent. This was natural, as Russia had more or less to start from scratch in respect to the basic equipment of heavy industries and transport. It was intended to change the emphasis from equipment to consumption, beginning with the third plan. But the intentions remained unfulfilled, as war preparations did not permit industrial diversion to consumers' goods. The emphasis on production goods as also on war goods has therefore continued. Before we go on to examine the relevance of the Russian economy to world economy, let us fix a fact which is often lost sight of in controversy. The possibility of planning an entire economy has now been established beyond a doubt. There have been partial breakdowns and bottlenecks in the Russian economy, but the gloomy forecasts of a total breakdown have been proved to be wholly groundless. That the Russian planning has been wise may be disputed; what can no more be disputed is that social management can plan and work out the entire economy of a country. A major capitalist weapon, that a country's economy cannot be run without the mechanism of interest and profits on capital, has been hopelessly blunted. Drafting the plan of an entire economy is quite in vogue now, not alone with socialists, but also with hard-headed capitalists, who naturally arrange to keep their capital intact and flourishing.

War is the greatest prevailing test of a nation's economy, and unless it can endure that, its achievements in other sphere do not last. The Soviet economy has stood this test. It may indeed be suggested that without American lend-lease and British assistance the Germans might perhaps have forced the Russians out of Stalingrad and Moscow and beyond, but it can as well be suggested that without the Russian effort the British economy and its capacity to wage war might have been placed in a precarious position. The Soviet economy has stood the stress of war as successfully as most other capitalist economies. It has indeed not been a prime motivation in the war. The prophecies of a war between capitalism and socialism have been due to an excessive rating of the strength of Soviet economy, and there is little likelihood that world capitalism will ever meet its doom in a war with the Russian socialism. Moreover, the manner in which the Russian economy has met the threat and actual ferocity of war is indistinguishable from that of any other capitalist economy. The reference here is not to the abandonment of the original anti-militarism of Lenin nor to the pursuit of foreign policies in the capitalist style. It is a purely economic fact that the Russian economy, admitting that war had to be prepared for, put its defence in heavy industries, big arms, and massed armies. The economic defence of Russia against war is the same as that of any major capitalist power. Whether any other defence is possible or not is here irrelevant, and the fact remains that similarity of pattern in the economic defence of capitalist and communist economies reduced Russia to the status of one participant among many, more or less powerful, but not a warring camp in itself. This similarity entails other consequences of foreign policy and alliances. On the basis, therefore, of its possible vitality as also its economic defence, the Russian economy is likely to remain as one participant among many, but never a host in itself so as to get into war against all the rest, much less to defeat them for a world victory of socialism.

The hopes as also the fears awakened by communist Russia have been far in excess of her actual strength. However much she may have deflected the thinking of capitalist powers and may yet continue doing so, her role in the war is subsidiary. Capitalism has continued to wage its wars, one member upon another, for whatever economic or moral reasons. Neither the strength of Russia nor the fear of it have been sufficiently strong to create a capitalist combination against her. It is possible that Russia may grow in strength and influence like any other power and, to the extent that she chooses to exercise political or economic pressure, may be a source of embarrassment to neighbouring capitalisms. However, the break-up of world capitalism, if it is to come, will come not as a result of war with a socialist power but out of happenings within the capitalist-imperialist structures themselves. With these happenings Russia has had nothing to do in an economic way, whatever may have been her political intervention through the Communist International.

The ferocity of the war on Russian soil has brought out a vital economic fact. As a result of the direct war destruction, but more so of the scorched-earth policy pursued by the two warring armies in their retreat, which is akin to the post-war incapacitation of a defeated economy, Russian productive capacity appears to have suffered severe losses. It is difficult to calculate the gaps caused by the destruction of the Dnieper Dam and of the group of industries around Dniepropetrovsk, together with such other loss of productive capacity in Leningrad and Stalingrad. One has only to recollect that the people were starved of consumers' goods so as to build up this productive equipment, and the process will in a considerable way have to be started again.[40] Large-scale equipment

40. The anti-imperialism of Russia will be severely tested on this issue. In the event of an outright victory, there will be great temptation to throw the burden of this non-immediately-productive activity on the backs of the defeated populations. This can be done through direct political control and in the form of indemnities or low-paid labour. It can also be achieved through establishing a town-village relationship in the exchange of goods with other East-European countries. Russian nationalism has already acquired the aggressive equipment of an exclusive national religion, a

(*Contd. …*)

of this character is liable to concentrated destruction. And yet there seem to have been two errors of foresight in the Russian plan. There is hardly a doubt that the Russian planners did not admit the possibility of an enemy penetrating five hundred miles and beyond into their industrial concentration to the west of the Volga. Moreover, adequate foresight does not seem to have been shown in respect to the dispersal of production. Under the stress of war and its aerial destruction, West Europeans are now evolving the concept of a single firm with the lowest economically feasible capacity in place of the firm with the maximum capacity. Small-scale production with small-unit techniques is becoming increasingly popular. It is difficult to say what part of a nation's basic equipment is capable of decentralization. But even as a measure of war, the Russian planners do not seem to have paid enough attention to this problem, and their large-scale industries have as such been liable to concentrated destruction.

What is now temporarily forced upon peoples as a war necessity appears, on other grounds, to be a necessary component of any national planning. In the measure that the advantages of heavy mechanization do not remain the restricted monopoly of a few peoples, and spread over from industry to agriculture, the problem of technics will assume a primary importance in economics. This problem could hitherto be slurred over, as the larger part of mankind and its largest occupation were kept in a state of dependence. With

---

militarist anthem, and a fine army with a lobe for extended defensive frontiers, and is developing other features with which we are not concerned here. Whether this nationalism will also persuade Russia to bring other populations into a town-village relationship economically, if not politically, is more than we can answer; the basis for it will be there and the temptation as well. Else, the Russian people will again, to some extent, have to be starved of consumers' goods. Incidentally, Russian activity in outer Mongolia and Sinkiang, in Poland and the Baltic State has shown such mixed features that whether it is imperialism for economic purpose or for defensive frontiers is difficult to say.

the conjoint mechanization of agriculture and industry that Russia is trying to put through, there must emerge large masses of men without occupation. As the objective of heavy mechanization is to go on shortening the time used in production, after a stage, the more a branch of industry or agriculture is mechanized and the larger the number of such branches, the greater will be the masses of men spewed out by these as necessary. As these men can stay in the old heavily mechanized industries only on condition that they produce for overseas markets or for war, Russia will probably at one stage or another enter into world trade on even more favourable conditions than those of West-European capitalisms. These men can also get absorbed into the vastly extended services of public health, education, and the like. It is even possible that new wants can be created, and thus, new industries to satisfy them. But the industries of these new wants and services may demand a new type of technics and the heavy mechanization of the old pattern may obstruct their emergence.[41] Unless, therefore, Russia starts producing in the not-too-distant future for overseas markets on a town-village relationship, her heavy mechanization may prove too rigid for a new pattern of technics, thus leading to the emergence of large masses in her own population as a new

41. Corresponding to this dispersal of production has taken place a like development in warfare. The importance of the small unit in the regular army and of guerillas has grown. These units are very lightly equipped with small arms and operate in groups of a few persons. Nevertheless, their action is complementary to the main movement of the massed-armies. They have shown the possibility of a new pattern of economic defence. But this possibility cannot be fully explored until a consciously planned economy chooses to experiment, not as a complementary but as a primary measure, with the small unit in production as also in warfare. Needless to say, these small units, in order to be effective over concentrated production and defence, must have all the advantages that science and technics can give them. It does not seem likely that the Russian economy will have any more creativity, than the West-European economies have the latitude, to pursue this conscious policy of small-unit technics as the primary, and the heavy mechanization as the secondary base.

submerged class of degraded humanity.[42]

There is indeed some substitutability in the produce of industrial plants; a plant that produces tractors can produce automobiles or tanks. But the range is not unlimited; a ship-building yard or an automobile plant cannot be turned into a factory for cement or bed-steads. In the Russian planning where whole blocks of demand have been given precedence over others, there is great danger that the comparative exhaustion of one set of demands coupled with the heavy mechanization of its industry may lead to serious maladjustment in changing over. There is also the possibility that heavy mechanization may check or even prevent the substitution of a new material for an old one; plastics may not replace iron or steel, even though this might mean loss of economic welfare. Even in a socialist economy, it would not be easy to scrap such heavy machinery as is the result of many years' labour. In addition, the lids on agricultural and on industrial consumption are different in nature; a man's demand for apparel is theoretically unlimited, while he cannot eat or drink beyond a certain quantity. For economies such as the Russian this is at present an academic point. But the effect may start showing after some decades of expanded and mechanized agriculture, and unless flexible techniques come to aid, serious maladjustment may as a result occur. It is doubtful if the Russians, with their dogma of heavy mechanization and unlimited expansion in the known fields, have paid enough attention to these various problems of substitution and change-over.

It must be emphasized that this problem of heavy mechanization in a socialist economy is not wholly similar to that under private management. Capital, under private

42. Such a class, apparently for political reasons, is already in existence. The numbers of men in the various labour camps of Siberia and elsewhere are sometimes estimated at millions. When the political reasons for the continuance of these labour camps have disappeared, it is doubtful if the economic reasons will not be as important. Besides labour camps, there is also the possibility of low and menial service.

ownership, has a double function. Its interests and profits serve, on the one hand, as a distribution mechanism for class-differentiations between the rich and the poor and, on the other, as a production mechanism for expansion and new development. A socialist economy does away with the distributive function of capital but it cannot avoid tackling and mastering its productive function. As an agent of production, capital with its numerous problems still remains in a socialist society. This capital is, of course, the saved labour of past years. But the problems raised by saved labour, which is concretized in heavy and intricate machinery, cannot be dismissed with the broad view that labour is the sole creator of value, and hence socialization of past labour puts an end to all difficulties. In a capitalist economy which is still not relegated, the operation of forces of stagnation and bankruptcy on the one hand and expansion on the other make for changes, some good, some bad, and enables the use of new inventions. What is left to the operation of these blind forces in a capitalist economy is taken over by conscious direction in a socialist economy. The responsibilities of this direction become immense and cannot be fulfilled merely by accounting and allotments or routine checking of the efficiency of one concern against another. Such a direction must be freed of all dogmas. The Russian objective to modernize in the manner of concentrated production of monopoly capitalism appears to be a dogma.[43] It makes for, as we have already seen, rigid

43. Unless information has been withheld, the Russian economy has not been too fruitful in the sphere of new inventions. There have indeed been projections and perfections of an old technique, and these may continue or increase. But no new items of economic welfare have been invented, no new industries created, no altering of an old industry into more pleasurable and healthful forms of labour. It is largely a copy of the best techniques available from West Europe and the United States. Perhaps it is too early to judge. In any case, Russian planning seems to give an impression of pursuit of statistics. A retarded economy must undoubtedly pursue expanded statistics of production, but there is just a possibility that such a pursuit of statistics may at some points militate against the pursuit of welfare. Let us take an imaginary example. A hundred-acre farm, with an

techniques, maladjustments in changeover, search for overseas markets or emergence of submerged classes, and an economic defence similar to that of capitalism. What it may mean to the ideal of socialist distribution we will presently examine. Even in the sphere of production, the rigid forms in which past labour is saved may act as a dead-weight. Socialist planning must treat these two entities of saved labour and current labour as distinct; whether one calls them capital and labour, or equipment and labour, is a secondary question. An over-all examination of the national equipment with its system of techniques necessitates the view that socialist planning does badly in taking over from late capitalism its production patterns; it must devise its own. Russian planning has been imitative; it has failed to devise patterns of production suited to a socialist ordering of economy.

We may now sum up the economic relevance, on the production side, of Russian economy to world capitalism. It has withdrawn nearly nine per cent of human race from the capitalist-imperialist web, but, as the dynamic that West-European capitalism extracted from a none too dependent pre-communist Russia was not great, the impact of such a withdrawal has not affected capitalism fundamentally. It is possible that Russia may after some time enter the world

---

optimum use of techniques, can be made to produce X quantity with the labour of a hundred persons. With the maximum use of heavy techniques and the quantity remaining unchanged, the labour on the farm can be cut down to fifty persons. The other fifty persons are drafted into making these heavy techniques possible, into mining coal and iron, into machine-manufacture, into transport. Production has thus registered an all-round increase; more agricultural production per head, more tonnage of iron, more mileage covered. Actually, however, there has been no real increase, X has remained X, and the other activity has been like the Jinn's going up and coming down. This is, of course, an extreme example but it illustrates the possibility of statistical expansion being merely a chimera. In actual life real expansion is interwoven with chimerical expansion, and an overall national planning must very carefully disentangle the one from the other and might even have to pursue a policy of healthful stability in certain directions.

market as a competitor of existing capitalisms; this will naturally harm them and cause their further decline. On the world-view, however, this will not abolish town-village relationships but will merely shift the areas of their operation. At the same time, planned production in Russia has established the possibility of planning and working out a nation's entire economy and has thus forged a propagandist item which causes constant irritation to capitalists. But its effect is not as great at it might have been, for the production patterns evolved by Russia do not show the way to abolish world poverty or world war. Her closed economy has aimed exclusively at internal reconstruction, and Russia has neither had the socialist fervour nor the capitalist need to face the issue of the diminishing yield of colonial economies.

On the distribution side, the Russia experience has brought into sharp relief the two distinct aspects of distribution as power and as wealth. However difficult it still is to express a categorical opinion on the distribution of wealth in Russia, there is no doubt as to the distribution of power and understanding. Power and wealth can be so wholly unrelated that an economy with an enormously maldistributed power can dole out a comparatively well-distributed wealth. The heavy mechanization of the Russian economy with its concentrated production is beyond the grasp of the common man in Russia. He has to depend on an elite for the management of this intricate mechanism as also for his general ideas regarding its internal and external needs. He has always to be told what his country needs internally and when and on what side to get into a war. His mental conditioning is the same as elsewhere; he has his broad ideas on patriotism and socialism and so forth; for their particular applications in specific situations, he has to depend wholly on an elite. Out of such a maldistributed understanding and the power that goes with it, a stateless society cannot arise. Whether a critical understanding, a ripened culture, and an over-all view can ever be imparted to the common man is another question; Russia with her centralized economic mechanism has not done so and cannot do so.

In respect to the distribution of wealth, let us briefly acquaint ourselves with the Marxian bases formulated from time to time without going too deeply into an argument that belongs elsewhere. The original formulation was, "from every one according to his capacity, to every one according to his needs." The first half is a straight formulation, for, aside from deliberate slackness, there is not much ambiguity about a person's capacity, and that too can be found out. The second half is an ambiguous formulation, for, which needs are here meant, the basically equal human needs of body and spirit or the conventional needs of various types of toilers? What again are these conventional needs? For that depends very much on one's standards of measurement, and these may approximate to basic equality. The formula was actually meant to convey the simple socialist faith of approximation to equal distribution of wealth, and if it was ambiguously worded that was perhaps an intellectual trick to use language which could bear a shifting economic argument. In its early stages, the Soviet economy tried zealously to work out this faith. Then came the medals and the stripes and the bits of ribbon. Finally came the formulation, announced as of transitional application, that everyone was to be paid according to his labour. If there were one single stream of produce and one simple block of work, a person's labour could be measured by the quantity either of the produce or the hours of work. In the mixed streams of modern production with its thousands different labour-processes such single-rod calculations are impossible. There must either be an arbitrary standard or the law of supply and demand will operate. Soviet economy has fixed a ceiling and a bottom within which wealth may be unevenly distributed on the usual economic basis of obtaining the best supply of different types of labour for corresponding scales of wages.

Broadly speaking, the bottom and the lid of this wage differentiation is around the ratio of 1 to 20. There are certain freak incomes, which are larger. These wages vary according to whether one is a single-process worker, a technician, an engineer, or a manager, according to industry, as between agriculture and industry, and even according to special performances in the arts and sciences and in civil services. There are also certain privileges attached to office in the Communist Party or in government service, which, whatever the grounds such as security and despatch on which they are conferred, make for a comfortable life. A fairly radical innovation is the institution of public bonds bearing interest. To dismiss these bonds as a device for making the citizen feel that his income is larger than his consumption would be to underrate the honesty or the self-confidence of the Soviet system. In a socialist economy such interest-bearing bonds have no purpose other than to create an exclusively personal stake of the citizen in the fortunes of his State. And in Russia today every citizen has acquired a stake in this State. But the rub comes in where the stake of some citizens is higher than that of certain others. These varying scales of interest-bearing patriotism must reflect themselves, in one wise or another, in some restricted laws of bequests. Already university education bears tuition fees. And yet to group together these wage, privilege, and stake differentiations as a class-formation would be to read more into the facts than is warranted. As long as Russia does not permit private ownership in the means of production, and there will have to be some sort of a revolution before this is done, formation of classes in the capitalist style cannot take place. Whether these wages and other differentiations will be dissolved or get stabilized will depend on the outcome of the clash between the production patterns of Soviet economy and the socialist faith of approximately equal distribution. The present tendencies are towards stabilization of difference.

These wage and other difference go to show that there are after all such things as higher and lower skills. But we have already seen that the concept of varying degrees of skill is highly illusory. What is not illusory is the concept of comparative scarcity. A rickshaw-driver's skill and use of muscle-power may be the same as, or even more than, those of a managerial performance at a desk, but the former can be had in a larger number of people than the latter. Some jobs will be scarcer than certain others; fewer persons will be able to do them, and a scarcity value will therefore always attach to them. This scarcity would also obtain in other spheres. The basic rent on land, for instance, is a property phenomenon, but the differential rent is an economic reality. Some plots of land would be more fertile than others or better located or abound in minerals. Moreover, there will always be a time-lag between the first user of a new item of comfort and the last, so that the occupation of newer built locations would be in a preferential position over others. This problem of comparative scarcity, therefore, as among different types of labour or among different sites would appear to endure in all economies. That it endures in Russia is not due to lack of will on the part of Soviet statesmen; they could not master it. For there can be no economic solution of these wage and comfort differentiations caused by comparative scarcity; there can only be an extra-economic faith. The socialist faith of approximation to equal distribution of wealth will ever have to master economic realities; it cannot come naturally out of them. To be effective, it cannot be a mere political imposition from without; it will have to devise its appropriate production patterns. Marxism has not attempted to evolve the production patterns suited to socialism, and it has weakened the human will behind the socialist faith of distribution by turning it into an automatic outcome of economic development. Socialist distribution is not the immanent law of a post-capitalist development; it is the result of an effort of will acting in unity with an appropriate economy.[44]

---

44. In passing, we may here refer to the violent swings of the Russian economic policy, occasioned partly by the varying concepts of socialist distribution. There was the early pure communism followed by the New Economic Policy of limited private ownership in production and trade. Then came the dizzy period of collective agriculture, followed once again by a kind of new economic policy in distribution with complete ownership in production.

(*Contd. …*)

Whatever our later examination of her political development may disclose to us, this rapid economic survey has made it clear that Russia is not likely to change into a stateless society nor is she the instrument of a socialist victory over capitalism. Her withdrawal from the capitalist system has not mortally affected it. As long as her production patterns, in particular her economic defence, remain what they are, her wage and power differentiations will continue, and she will be unable to show the way to abolition of the state or of world poverty and wars. What she has demonstrated is the possibility of planned economy under social ownership and of the tremendous power that a retarded nation may speedily achieve. The war with Germany has also steeled the Russians into a powerful nation, for whose hand of friendship other States would be eager. From this may flow influences of good or evil import, but the prime actors of world history will have to be searched for elsewhere.

[1943]

Despite these swings, Russian economic expansion has proceeded with a good speed, in some ways better than the best American speed. The Russian expansion is not questioned nor its speed, and we are not directly concerned here with the political ruthlessness that has gone with it; the only question is whether this same speed, or even better, could not have been attained by a more consistent and continuous policy. Perhaps the first land to come under social ownership had to go through these experiences. Perhaps, also, some violent swings of policy are unavoidable when private property is beaten into a social shape. One has, therefore, to beware of superficial criticisms of Russia and of the mere analogies now so popularly drawn between the Russian and the West-European economies. Only such critical understanding of Russia has meaning as reinforces the need for social ownership and as is informed by the desire to extract certain over-all principle for the planning of a socialist economy. And here the Russian experience has shown that progress can have two rates, an optimum rate and an intermittently ruthless rate. The optimum rate of progress may actually be more revolutionary than a ruthless rate.